MARGY

I AM
ENOUGH

From depression, anxiety,
and addiction to recovery

I Am Enough: From depression, anxiety, and addiction to recovery
© Margy Jackson 2021

ISBN: 978-1-922532-36-7 (Paperback)
        978-1-922532-37-4 (eBook)

 A catalogue record for this book is available from the National Library of Australia

Editors: Kristy Martin and Beverley Streater
Cover Design: Ocean Reeve Publishing
Design and Typeset: Ocean Reeve Publishing
Printed in Australia by Ocean Reeve Publishing and Clark & Mackay Printers

Published by Margy Jackson and Ocean Reeve Publishing
www.oceanreevepublishing.com

Dedication

This book is dedicated to the loves of my life.
Mum and my children J & A.
You never stopped believing in me.
Love you always.

Contents

Introduction

I Am Enough is a true account of my struggle through anxiety and depression, leading to my alcohol dependence, sexual abuse, domestic violence, and fractured relationships.

I Am Enough is also a story of joy through music, courage, bravery, and resilience; overcoming low self-esteem to ultimately stand up and say 'Enough' and use my voice to speak up.

I have changed many names in my book to protect people's privacy due to the nature of the subject material. I would like to thank my friends and family for allowing me to share my treasured memories and to write about less happy events.

I hope that my story will empower other women to begin to tell their stories. It is through our sharing of experiences that we can support each other and instigate change. Nothing changes if nothing changes.

It is time to collectively use our voices to say #ENOUGH: We will be seen and heard.

For all the women out there who don't feel they have a voice, I believe you.

Georgy Jackson
2021.

Endorsements

Margy Jackson's voice in her beautiful memoir is the perfect mix of honesty, vulnerability, wisdom, warmth, and power. Anyone seeking courage and hope to inspire them on their own journey will find it in *I Am Enough*.

—Annie Grace, author of *This Naked Mind* and
The Alcohol Experiment

This book is a great insight of the journey of one young woman from the southwest of Victoria into the mist of alcohol dependence and all the troubles that come along with that descent but more importantly provides a story of hope that change is not only possible but is better than one can imagine for themselves. When one is looking through the mist of alcohol, it's hard to really believe change is possible.

Whilst it is one woman, the elements of the story resonate with many women who have struggled with dependence on this drug called alcohol. I have worked in this sector for many years and whilst no two experiences are the same, there are similarities that will resonate with people and importantly it also provides a vision of hope. Issues such as 'trying to fit in', 'rebellion against parents or authority', 'experience of trauma', 'need to self-medicate away emotions yet only to find they come back worse and stronger the next day', and the years of torment that this thinly disguised 'friend' called alcohol provides. I am so glad to have met the author and to see how she has been able to take charge and see for herself the need to change and more importantly the wonders a life free from alcohol can provide. Recovery is not just about stopping the substance of dependence, it's about building a life where alcohol no longer fits in. I hope all who read this book find some inspiration and wisdom from Margy's personal story.

—Mark Powell, Operations Manager WRAD (Western Region Alcohol and Drug Centre)

Frequently whilst trying to help control depressive and anxiety symptoms, we see a reliance on alcohol presenting as a coping mechanism for underlying past traumas. This book shows, no matter where we are on life's journey, there is always hope and the time for positive change.

—Dr Clare Mooney MBChb, DRCOG

A bravely honest and moving memoir that will transform lives.

—Clare Pooley, author of *The Sober Diaries*

Congratulations Margy!

One courageous woman standing up to tell her story to the world will create global ripples, empowering others to do the same and join #ENOUGH.

This story will set off lightbulbs for all of us struggling to make sense of not who we are but WHY we are.

—Dr Vicki Gardner, BAppSc(Chiro), Certified NeuroEmotional Practitioner

Chapter 1
Growing up in 1970s Australia

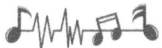

The 1970s were an interesting period to go through puberty in Australia. It was a time of change. As a child, I was aware of the 'cultural cringe' of being an Aussie. The Australian accent was mocked on TV, and I felt that Australia wasn't a player on the world stage at this time. Gough Whitlam was prime minister due to the success of the Labor Party's 'It's Time' campaign in 1972. Australian men over the age of eighteen were being conscripted to fight in the Vietnam War, Paul Hogan was advertising Winfield Cigarettes, *Skippy the Bush Kangaroo* was on TV and Mrs Marsh was using Palmolive dishwashing liquid to soak her hands in.

My parents were 'ten-pound Poms', a scheme run by the Australian Government after the second world war to attract people from the UK to emigrate to Australia. It provided UK citizens with a ten-pound fare to Australia if they agreed to remain in Australia for two years after arrival or refund the cost of their assisted passage.

Mum's family, including my nanna, poppa, aunty, uncle, and mum, sailed from Southampton in England in 1955 to make a new life in Australia. They had left their home in Shetland to sail across the world to Melbourne. My poppa's brother had already emigrated to Australia several years before this and my mum's family were going to live with him in the small, coastal town of Warrnambool in Southwest Victoria.

My dad was from Kirkcaldy, in Fife, Scotland. He was the eldest son in a family of nine sisters and one brother. He was tired of the cold, miserable weather in Scotland and decided to emigrate to 'sunny Australia'. He also sailed from Southampton, arriving in Melbourne just before the Olympic Games in 1956. He wasn't keen on the hustle and bustle of Melbourne and asked his immigration officer if he knew of a place near the sea that was quiet and picturesque. The immigration officer pursed his lips, after asking Dad to repeat what he said because of his broad Scottish accent, thought carefully for a minute and said, 'That sounds like Warrnambool.' Dad took his advice, jumped on a train at Spencer Street Station and headed off to Warrnambool at the end of the train line.

Joe started working as a plumber at the Warrnambool Base Hospital. My poppa was a carpenter by trade and was also working at the base hospital at the time. He met Dad by chance one day, came home to Nanna, and said, 'I met a braw young chap fae Fife, Scotland, deday Mam, can I invite him aroond fae mince and tatties?' (Aussie translation: G'day love, I met a ripper young bloke from Fife, Scotland today; can I invite him around for a tinnie and a snag?) Nanna was keen to meet a fellow Scot and Dad was invited to join my mum's family for dinner.

My mum was a quiet, shy, young lass. She had been born deaf, as my nanna had contracted German measles when she was pregnant with Mum. On arrival in Australia, Mum went to the Victorian School for the Deaf in Melbourne. She found this very challenging as it was so different from her deaf school in Aberdeen in Scotland. She wasn't happy at her new school in Melbourne and returned home. She started working at the Warrnambool Woollen Mill which was just across the Merri River from their new home that my poppa was building at number one MacDonald Street.

Poppa gave Dad the job of putting in the plumbing at the new house. Dad was quite smitten with the lovely, shy, young lass he glimpsed from time to time while he was laying the new pipes. He worked up the courage to ask Mum to a dance at the Warrnambool Town Hall and Mum accepted. She was very enamoured with this handsome, young Scottish plumber, and they started courting.

Mum and Dad married on 1 July 1961 at the St John's Presbyterian Church in Warrnambool. A *most* auspicious date as it was also Dad's thirty-first birthday *and* the same day that Princess Diana was born. Mum was only twenty years old, so there was a ten-year age gap between them. Nanna and Poppa had given Mum and Dad the block of land next to their place as an engagement present. Dad set about building our family home at number three MacDonald Street, with help from my pop. The newlyweds lived with my grandparents for several months, moving into their new home just in time for Mum to celebrate her twenty-first birthday in October 1961.

Mum returned to her factory job at the Warrnambool Woollen Mill, just across the Merri River from home and Dad took a plumbing position at the Fletcher Jones factory.

I was born in May 1963, my younger sister, Jane, in April 1965 and my brother, Allan, in September 1967. My upbringing was happy, full of singing, laughter, and fun times with my family.

Dad's parents, Margaret and Joe Jackson, sailed out to Australia to visit us from Scotland in 1967 and stayed with us for several months. I had been named after my granny, and I adored her. Granddad was quite a strict and stern man, and I recall going for a walk with him one day when I was only three years old. We ended up nearly walking around the whole of Warrnambool. He held my hand very tightly, and I was too scared of him to protest, so I just kept walking.

I was a bright student, and I could read before I went to school. I recall being in the car with Mum and Dad and driving past a petrol station near our house. This station had a big *BP* sign above the building. I pointed at it when I was about three and said, 'Look, Mummy, *BP Pick-a-Box*,' which was a game show on TV at the time.

I loved primary school, and I remember running ahead of Mum and Jane on my first day because I could not wait to start.

I was prone to moodiness, though, and I had a bad temper. I have always been fiercely independent, and I liked to get my own way. I have asked Mum whether my anger and tantrum-throwing was because of her deafness and me being left in my cot for long periods to cry when she couldn't hear me. She said, 'No,' but I think this early trauma did affect my anxious behaviour from a young age. Jane, my younger sister, has always said that I have 'high highs' and 'low lows'. Jenny Valentish, in her book *Woman of Substances*, states:

> In comment sections across the internet, the battle rages eternal as to whether drug-takers (and I include alcohol) are mad, bad or sad. The research is clear. A toxic combination of temperamental traits and environmental stress efficiently turns some people into a time bomb for addiction.

My clock had begun to tick.

Dad was the boss in our house and if he said 'no' then you could not change his mind. I was a stubborn and wilful little girl, and we would lock horns from time to time. As the eldest son in a Scottish family with nine sisters, Dad was used to being admired and spoiled. My Scottish granny had doted on Dad and, apparently, she had 'taken to her bed' for two weeks when Dad told her he was emigrating to Australia. He was the 'golden boy' and could do no wrong. All of Dad's family were quite shocked when he decided to leave Scotland and move to the other side of the world.

Our Warrnambool family home in MacDonald Street was at the end of a cul-de-sac, over a small hill. We spent lots of time with the neighbourhood kids riding our bikes up and down the hill. There was gravel at the bottom of the hill near our driveway and we were careful not to ride into it for fear of losing control of our bikes and ending up with gravel rash.

Our place was a white and grey, 1960s-style, single-storey, conite, three-bedroomed house. It had a large window in the front lounge room, to make the most of the scenic view of the Merri River. There was an elevated, enclosed porch on the left side of our house that Dad loved to sit in to read the paper. In later years, I used to chuckle when I drove up the driveway and saw the back of Dad's bald head above his recliner rocker in the front porch, the newspaper open and footrest cranked up.

The neighbourhood gang liked to play down near the river, much to Mum and Nanna's dismay. 'Noo bairns, byde awaa fae da burn or you'll aw faa in an droond', Nanna would say to us many times. ('Now kids, stay away from the water or you will all fall in and drown.') We dared each other to walk across the river on stepping-stones under the car bridge or jump from the footbridge downstream a bit to a grassy mound underneath, as a prerequisite for joining the 'gang'. Our neighbour, Joanne, from two doors up was an only child and we would all pal around together, having 'clubs' in our playhouse that Dad built in our backyard and putting on musical performances for the neighbours. I even made a stage curtain that we could open from one of Mum's old sheets.

We had a gate between our house and our grandparents', so we could have easy access between the two properties.

I have a treasured series of photos taken of Joanne, Jane, and I standing in front of fences at Nanna and Poppa's or our place. We call these pics 'the fence photos' as they document our growth from tiny girls to teenagers and young women. Joanne didn't have any grandparents, so she was happily adopted by Nanna and Poppa and she loved them dearly.

Nanna was a formidable woman, always three steps ahead of us, and did not take any nonsense from anyone. Poppa was a very kind man and I can still see him sitting in his chair in his overalls and favourite woollen jumper beside their slow combustion stove in the kitchen, a cup of tea in hand. Nanna ruled the roost, though, and if you decided to do something that she didn't like, you better look out. But she was a very kind person and helped many people when they were sick or needed company. Dad used to call these people 'Kitty's lame ducks'.

I went to South Warrnambool Primary School, which was a five-minute walk from home, and loved it. I knew everyone and I felt that I was 'someone' at primary school. I was the only student from my year six class to go to Warrnambool High School. The whole six of my classmates went to the local tech college, Caramut Road Tech, as it was known then. So I was alone, scared, anxious, and miserable on orientation day. There was no primary-to-secondary transition program in those days.

Dad dropped me off out the front of my new high school on orientation day in December 1974 and I considered bolting and running away. Not being a quitter, I made myself get out of the car and walk up the path. My legs were trembling, and I was terrified. The bulk of the other new students were from the three other main primary schools in town. I sat on a bench by myself and heard a kid say, 'Check out the daggy purple flares and paper lunch bag; must be a country kid.' I knew he was talking about me, and I wanted to just shrivel up and die. It was an awful introduction to my high school years, one I never recovered from.

I was euphoric every Friday night coming home on the bus—no school for two whole days. On Monday mornings, I looked like I was going to a funeral. My anxiety about going to school would start mid-Sunday afternoon and progressively worsen until I slowly dragged myself up the hill and got on the bus. I would usually sit by myself, gazing out the window and trying to calm my nerves before another week of horror began.

This seesaw of emotions continued to plague me and prevented me from settling into my new school. At my primary school, we had been trusted and spoken to respectfully by our teachers. At high school, it seemed like the teachers were always waiting for us to stuff up so they could punish us. I would have knots in my stomach most of the time and I didn't have anyone that I felt comfortable talking to about this. I didn't realise at the time that my anxiety was unusual or uncommon. I thought that I just felt things more than most other people, and that going through puberty was exacerbating my feelings. Nowadays, I know that my symptoms were quite serious and those around me would've suggested counselling or seeing a psychologist. There is also a history of depression and anxiety in my family, and this certainly was evident in my behaviour.

In May 1975, my family sailed back to the UK for a six-month trip to visit our relatives in England and Scotland. I had just started high school and my teachers were concerned that I might fall behind. I remember Dad coming up to school and having a chat with the Year Seven coordinator about this. Mr. Scarf explained to Dad that I would need to be prepared to repeat the year. This added to my anxiety once again, as I had already struggled through a huge transition from primary school to secondary school and I didn't like the idea of doing it twice.

We sailed to Great Britain on the SS *Australis*. It was a huge ocean liner, with two main restaurants, the 'Atlantic' and 'Pacific', a cinema, a large shopping arcade, and several pools on the promenade deck. Jane, Allan, and I had a ball running all over the ship and having an extended holiday from school. The kids ate earlier than the adults at a special early dining sitting and when I wasn't spewing over the side of the ship we would go to our table and always order 'cold cuts' because we loved chicken.

I had my twelfth birthday crossing the International Date Line and therefore it was my birthday for two whole days. This would've been brilliant apart from the fact that I had chronic sea sickness and spent much of my time throwing up. I had always been prone to motion sickness while travelling in cars and I even felt nauseous on swings and carousels.

I had been a chubby pre-teen and often teased for being so, but I lost a lot of weight on that trip. I was so ill that I begged Dad to let me fly on to my relatives in England when we disembarked at the various ports we visited. Dad wasn't keen on that idea and took me to the ship's doctor, who gave me an injection of something in the bum to stop me vomiting. I was seriously dehydrated after being laid up in my bunk onboard for a week. I toughed it out and arrived in Southampton much thinner five weeks later.

We drove up the M6 to Scotland and arrived in Kirkcaldy, Fife, in June 1975. We spent three months living with my granny in her 'wee hoose' in Balfour Street. In between visiting all of Dad's sisters and their families, we would take Granny and her little poodle, Kim, out sightseeing in the little red van that Dad had borrowed from his brother-in-law. We all squished in the van and toured around having cups of tea and sing-a-longs all over Scotland. One day, Granny had wound the window down for some fresh air and I looked out my window and saw Kim swinging on her lead. 'Dad, stop the car! Kim has jumped out the window', I yelled. Dad quickly pulled into a side road and poor Kim was rescued, a little shaken but not injured.

'Och aye, yee wee bizom, I canna tak ma een off yee', said Granny while hugging her precious pet. We drove up to the highlands, even spending a night camped in the van beside Loch Ness. Dad had the whole front seat to himself, while Mum, Jane, Allan and I were all squashed together in the back seat. I was shitting myself that the Loch Ness Monster would come and eat us all and sat there wide awake all night keeping a lookout. It was a very uncomfortable night, and we were all very grumpy and tired the next day.

I loved being in Scotland with my family during that trip. I just felt more 'at hame' there with my wee Scottish granny, aunties, and cousins. I used to snuggle up on the couch with Granny and watch *Little House on the Prairie*, often not even accompanying my immediate family when they went out for trips in the red van. Granny loved her 'sweeties' and always had a special treat for us 'bairns' from her sweetie jar. We sang lots of songs in Granny's lounge room, ate countless fish-and-chip suppers, drank hundreds of cups of tea and I felt secure and happy basking in the bosom of my 'ain folk'. We even went to school with one of my cousins as they were going on an excursion to Edinburgh Zoo, and we were invited to go as well. I recall standing up in front of the class and answering questions about Australia and what it was like living 'down under'. The Scottish kids were in fits of laughter because of our Aussie accents. I decided not to speak after the Scottish kids started calling me 'Skippy' and doing the tongue noises. Yes, *Skippy* was on TV in Scotland at the time as well, and all the Scottish kids thought that kangaroos jumped down main streets in Australia or that we all had them as pets.

We caught the North Sea ferry from Aberdeen to Lerwick in Shetland to spend two weeks with Mum's relatives. I was seasick as usual, and it was a very rough voyage. We stayed in the first house that Poppa had built, called 'The Sparl', which was right beside a burn (lake). We had to get out of the car and climb over the fence with our bags and walk to the house which had no indoor plumbing or electricity. We were fascinated staying here in this old-fashioned place with Poppa's sister, Aunty Katie, and her granddaughter, Brenda. We were the first Aussies that Brenda had ever encountered, and we taught her to say Aussie slang like 'G'day mate' and 'She'll be right' and then laugh at how weird it sounded when she said it. Brenda was a terrific sport, though, and we became firm friends. I loved Shetland and its wild beauty, kind and gentle people, and smoked haddock. Saying farewell at the ferry terminal to return to mainland Scotland was heartbreaking. I told my new friend Brenda that I would be back.

I was very reluctant to return to Australia in September 1975. Our three months had flown by very quickly and I started scheming with my Scottish cousins about being allowed to remain behind and live in Scotland. Of course, this was met with a stern 'Get in the car' from Dad. I just couldn't face going back to being a loner at a school I hated. I turned and faced the window and cried back down the M6 to Oxford in England, tears streaming down my face. I didn't speak to anyone, and I felt like my heart was going to break. I vowed that I would return to Scotland as soon as I was old enough to travel by myself.

I had written a note to my future self, full of sadness and despair at having to leave, and shoved it down a gap behind Granny's loo. I didn't tell anyone that I had done this, and my twelve-year-old self thought it was a great way of ensuring that I would return.

I hung around with the tough kids on the ship on the way back to Australia. I was cross with Mum and Dad for making me return to Australia. I decided to befriend the tough kids to annoy Mum and Dad. I had never been naughty with my friends before, but I decided in my twelve-year-old petulance to become quite obnoxious. We once again sailed on the SS *Australis,* and this time my sea legs seemed to kick in and I wasn't so sick. There was a soda bar where the teenagers hung out and I started chatting to them. They were a bit older than me and smoked and hung around at the ship's disco. I started having a few puffs of my new friends' smokes and I thought I was very cool and sophisticated. I begged Mum to let me go to the disco which didn't start until after ten o'clock and I was given permission—providing that Mum came with me to make sure I didn't get up to too much mischief. I loved dancing to 'Moonlighting' by Leo Sayer under the sparkling glitter ball.

It was quite strange that I seemed to have found my sea legs, as the return voyage to Australia was very rough. I can recall ropes being strung along the passageways for people to grab onto when the ship listed. Dad said that at one dinner sitting, his chair slid across the dining room floor when the ship hit a huge wave, and he looked up to see that he was sitting at a new table. A tragedy occurred when the elevator doors opened unexpectedly, and a passenger fell to her death down the lift shaft. I remember reading about this in the *Herald Sun* newspaper when we returned home.

I loved disembarking at new and exotic ports. I recall being on a rather dilapidated old bus in Las Palmas, tearing around a narrow road on a steep hill and clinging on to the seat in front of me for dear life. We went to the San Francisco Church which has a golden shrine, and I stood there in awe looking at the intricate carvings and exquisite craftmanship. In Cape Town, South Africa we took a walk around the city centre and hopped on a bus, only to be asked to get off, as this bus was only for black people. This was the first time I had ever encountered racial discrimination and Dad had to explain what apartheid meant. I decided that this was a very unfair system, and it ignited my sense of justice. This trip around the world was the beginning of my lifelong love of travel and delight at experiencing new cultures and places.

We arrived back in Australia in October 1975 and Joanne, my next-door neighbour and good pal, couldn't believe that I had grown up so much in six months.

Chapter 2
Relationships

When I reluctantly returned to high school in October 1975, all the kids had formed their friendship groups by this stage, and I just 'floated' around from group to group like an outsider. I was very unhappy at having to return to a school I didn't like and wanted to go back to Scotland. I continued to study hard, and I found schoolwork easy after seeing the world firsthand. Instead of having to repeat the year, I received an academic award for obtaining such high marks.

Once again, I befriended the tough kids and started smoking in the toilets and being quite obnoxious at home. 'Come up to the loo for a smoke at recess, Margy—everyone does it; just look out for Old Hag,' referring to one of the senior teachers that we thought looked like a witch. So, every morning recess and lunchtime I went to the loos and smoked. How we didn't get caught I will never know, as the smoke used to billow out underneath the toilet doors. I befriended a tall, red-headed lass called Elizabeth, and we met up in the loos and smoked every day. Joanne and I would sneak off down to the riverbank and smoke after school, rubbing our hands on leaves and grass so that our mums couldn't smell the smoke.

At home, I shared a room with my sister, Jane. We were close, but she wasn't as tidy as me, and I became quite fixated on everything being tidy and in its place. So, we had an imaginary line that went down the middle of our bedroom and my side was very tidy and hers wasn't. I knew that she worried about my wild behaviour and didn't like my smoking or who I was hanging around with. She told me so, but I carried on regardless of what anyone thought.

I think my reactive behaviour was in response to not having control over being allowed to stay in the UK. I was intentionally being difficult so that Dad and Mum might reconsider sending me back to Scotland where I had been happier. I even wrote a letter to my aunty and uncle in Wheatley asking them if I could come and stay with them because I was so unhappy at school.

Being tidy gave me some physical control over my surroundings. I became fussy with my food as well, and many evening meals would end up thrown over my grandparents' fence. I liked people commenting on how thin I had become. This became an obsession too, and I was determined never to be called chubby again.

School was still a place I disliked, but I got through it by being a good student. I was class captain and a member of the Student Representative Council. One ordinary day, a male friend of mine who was also a long-time family friend returned to class after lunch looking dishevelled. I said something along the lines of, 'Tough footy match today?'

He replied, 'Yeah, you could say that.'

I found out many years later that he had been defending my honour because the class smart arse had been telling everyone that he'd 'had his way' with me!

I was still hanging around with the tough kids and one Saturday morning we were in town shopping. They all used to shoplift regularly and dared me to take some cosmetics and hair dye from a department store. I made sure no-one was looking and shoved the stuff into my bag. I tried to walk casually out of the store and made it to the arcade where I was tapped on the shoulder by a security guard. I took off like Raelene Boyle in the hundred metres final and didn't stop running until I got home. I spent the rest of that day wearing sunglasses and a scarf over my head, terrified that the cops would come around and arrest me for stealing. I decided that day that I never wanted to steal again and put the stuff in a brown paper bag and threw it in a public bin.

On the weekends, my tough girlfriends hung around at various teenage hangouts. One Sunday, they invited me to come along. I went to meet them at the kiosk near Ocean Beach Caravan Park. Mum told me to be home by lunchtime in time for our Sunday roast. Jane came with me, to keep an eye on me I think, and started getting worried when lunchtime approached. She said, 'Come on, Margy, we have to go home.' I wouldn't go with her, so she left and ran home by herself.

We walked to the bowling alley, a regular haunt of teenagers in our town, and played the pinball machines for a while. After some time had passed and we were getting bored, one of the girls said, 'Let's go to the barrel,' so I went with my friends. Barrels were very common in the 1970s. A barrel of beer would be purchased, and everyone would chip in to pay for it. They were usually held in backyards, and everyone would stay and drink until the barrel was empty, cheering when the last beer made the barrel tap whistle.

I was fourteen and I started drinking beer. I recall not liking the taste of it much, but I didn't want to appear uncool. After a couple, I felt quite lightheaded but kept drinking. After five or six glasses of beer, I felt sick, and the yard was spinning. 'I might just lie down for a minute', I slurred as one of my *friends* took me into the house and I threw up in the toilet. I went to lie down on a bed in one of the bedrooms and fell asleep. When I woke up, another three or four people were lying on the bed. We all lay there chatting for a while and I knew that it was way past five o'clock by this stage, but I didn't want to go home.

One of the guys lying on the bed invited me to go back to his place. I thought he was attractive with his blue eyes and surfy blonde hair and agreed to go with him. We must have walked to his house, and he took me to a bus parked in the backyard. I was a very naive, fourteen-year-old virgin, and I didn't realise that it wasn't a good idea to go into the bus with a guy I didn't know. He led me to a bed up the back and we lay down and kissed. Before I realised what was happening, he was on top of me, pulling up my skirt and unzipping his jeans. I didn't even have the presence of mind to struggle. I just froze. He penetrated me and I felt a stab of pain and cried out. He looked a bit startled and jumped up. I felt between my legs and there was blood. I was very scared and shocked and started sobbing.

I ended up getting home around nine in a taxi that night. Mum and Jane were beside themselves with worry. I was hungover, sick, anxious, and miserable. I concocted a story about cooking something at my friend's place and getting sick. Mum and Dad didn't buy it and went next door and got my nanna, who was a nurse, to come and have a look at me. I recall her looking into my eyes with a torch and asking me if I had taken something like drugs or alcohol. I told her that I had been smoking and that it had made me feel sick. I also remember throwing my stained undies into our slow combustion stove to burn because I couldn't face looking at them. I didn't tell anyone what had happened, and this story has stayed tucked inside my brain until now.

*

That last bit was extremely hard to write, and I have had to stop for a while. I have been sitting in my chair in the lounge room feeling relieved that I have finally laid this burden down. It has never occurred to me in the forty-three years since this happened that it wasn't my fault. I have blamed myself for being stupid and naive. I have carried this guilt around all this time, and it is such a relief to finally tell this story.

I have seen many psychologists in the past twenty years or so to determine why my self-esteem was so low. I feel so sad for younger me and how making a stupid decision to bow to peer group pressure and drink alcohol led to giving away such a precious gift. I have such an ache in my heart, as I genuinely believed that it was my fault that I was raped.

Considering the details now, there can be no doubt that it was rape. There was no violence involved, but I didn't give my consent, I was underage, and I was affected by alcohol. Considering this now with my adult brain, I would have to concede that it was also premeditated, as the guy asked me to accompany him and took me to the bus. I believe this enormous trauma and subsequent escapism into alcohol was the catalyst for my low self-worth.

Home life was quite strained for some time after this. I was very worried that I could be pregnant, and I lived for a couple of weeks in total fear. I was thinking, *Shit, I'm too young to have a baby; Dad will kick me out; I will have to leave school; how will I afford to live? I won't be able to finish my studies and go on to uni; no-one will want me because I am soiled goods*, and on and on the voices in my head went.

Every morning and afternoon after school, I would rush to the loo to see if my period had started. I don't know how I went to school and acted 'normal'. I did get my period, thank God, and life continued as usual.

Dad and I didn't speak much after this episode, and I tried to avoid him whenever possible. I just felt so worthless, guilty, and cheap. There were about two years during this time where we rarely acknowledged each other, and it was painful.

As I mentioned earlier, my dad had been brought up in a large Scottish family, with nine sisters and one brother, and Granddad ruled his family with an iron fist. My aunties have told me that if they came downstairs with makeup on to go out, my granddad would stop them and growl, 'Your ney goin onywhar wee dat muck on yer face, ye look like a hoor, gee up the stair and wash it off.' Aussie translation: 'You are not going anywhere with that muck on your face, you look like a whore, go upstairs and wash it off.' This type of parenting didn't work on me, and I either fired up or cut Dad off when we came to loggerheads.

I bawled my eyes out for two days when he wouldn't let me go to see the rock band Sherbet at the Warrnambool Town Hall in 1976. I don't think I have ever cried that much. I ranted and raved and begged Dad to let me go. All my school friends were going, and I was very upset. When Dad made up his mind and said, 'No,' nothing would convince him otherwise. My tantrums just made his resolve all the stronger. I was so upset and cross I tried climbing out my bedroom window, but he had nailed the flyscreens on. He was a very clever man!

At odds with my 'break all the rules' persona was my determination to do well at school. I had an abject fear of failure and I always strove for top marks. I continued smoking, drinking, and being wild and balanced it out by being a top student. I was seeking approval from my dad, who had been dux of his school and expected us to achieve this as well. I studied hard to obtain his approval, but I always felt like I didn't quite measure up.

Chapter 3
The fire in the belly

When I was young, I'd listen to the radio
Waitin' for my favourite songs
When they played, I'd sing along
It made me smile.

This is the first verse of *Yesterday Once More* by The Carpenters. Music has comforted me in my saddest times, added joy to my happiest times, and soothed me when I was tired and broken. Without it, my world would be a sad, grey, ugly place. I love this song because it reminds me so much of happy times singing with my dad and Jane. We performed quite a lot and Dad was a fantastic singer. He would often sing to his customers after he finished a plumbing job which is quite a unique and entertaining 'extra service' for a plumber, I think.

When I was in primary school, we listened to a weekly radio program called *Let's Join In*. I remember hearing 'Blowin' in the Wind' by Bob Dylan for the first time and being strongly influenced by the message of peace in his song. I realised that music was a very powerful way of expressing your feelings and beliefs. I can recall watching the Academy Awards on TV in 1973 and seeing a very young Michael Jackson performing the song 'Ben'. The hair stood up on the back of my neck watching him sing and the passion in his voice just moved me. I would cry listening to Roy Orbison singing 'Crying' and I loved the melancholy vibe in the song 'The Air That I Breathe' by The Hollies.

Our family belonged to the very small Presbyterian Church in our neighbourhood that held a concert every year. When I was about ten I heard two girls singing and playing the guitar together at this concert and I thought, *Yes, I am going to learn how to play the guitar.* Santa brought me my first guitar for Christmas that year and I set about teaching myself how to play it. There was no question of getting paid lessons because we weren't that sort of family. I sat on my bed for hours at a time inventing chords and trying to play simple tunes. I taught myself how to play 'Morningtown Ride' by The Seekers using chords I had made up.

I have always had a very good ear for music and I just experimented with different fingers on strings until the chord sounded okay. My uncle, a guitar player, realised that I was quite musical, and he gave me lessons and taught me the basic chords. He took me with him to the Country and Western Club in Kepler Street, Warrnambool one Sunday afternoon in 1973 where he was a member. I was asked to get up and sing, so I nervously stood up on the stage. I sang 'Banks of the Ohio' and it was the first time I had sung into a microphone. I felt like Olivia Newton-John and I belted the song out. I fell in love with performing on stage that day.

I loved nothing better than sitting on my bed strumming away and playing my favourite songs. Sometimes I would stand out in the front garden on a wall beside the lounge room window and belt out 'Delta Dawn' by Helen Reddy or 'If Not for You' by Olivia Newton-John. I would do this just as the Warrnambool Woollen Mill workers were leaving for the day to get feedback from a captive audience. I loved singing and performing; it was my happy place. I have been reading Linda Ronstadt's *Simple Dreams* autobiography and she says that she could *feel* the music and I totally understood that. Music could lift me to ecstatic heights or reduce me to tears. There is no other medium as powerful as music.

I sang in the Caledonian Choir with my siblings and the children of our Scottish friends. We rehearsed every Friday evening in the Cally Club Rooms before the senior choir rehearsed. Our choir leader and pianist was a lady called Cath Brymer who was very involved with the theatre company and music in Warrnambool at that time. She took a bit of an interest in me and frequently told me, 'Margy, can you sing a bit quieter please?'

I was given a solo to do at the upcoming Haggis Supper which was a big annual event for the Scottish community. My nanna always did the traditional ode, called 'The Ode to the Haggis', and it was a big deal for me to be chosen to sing a solo. A single light was shining on my choir gown, and I wore a tartan sash over my shoulder as I belted out the words from 'He':

> *He can touch a tree and turn the leaves to gold, he knows*
> *every lie that you and I have told. Though it makes him sad*
> *to see the way we live, he'll always say, 'I forgive'.*

The room went totally quiet after I'd finished singing and then people started clapping. I knew that I had nailed it, although I was only eleven years old. I was so euphoric, I wanted to go on singing forever. I remember thinking, *This is what I want to do*. Artists refer to this feeling as 'the fire in the belly'.

One Saturday night in 1977 when I was supposed to be at the movies, I invited some of the 'cool' kids from high school over to my house for a party. We got stuck into Mum and Dad's liquor cabinet and I got out my guitar and played a couple of songs. Mum and Dad were out at the Cally Club and I had to tear around and clean the place up before they got home. I didn't do a particularly good job and they thought that the house had been broken into. I have never owned up to this, so I guess the cat's out of the bag now! Can you still be grounded when you are fifty-eight? I am sorry, Mum.

One of the guys who had been at the party was a drummer and he and a few mates were starting a band and looking for a singer. He told his mate that he had heard me sing and that I was good. I was invited to audition for a place in the band and I got the job and I can remember playing 'Lying in the Arms of Mary' by The Sutherland Brothers and 'Quiver'. I was excited, but I thought that there would be no way that Dad would let me join a boys' rock band at fourteen years of age.

Standing in the lounge room, back to the heater, in front of Dad and asking if I could join the band was nerve-racking. He was sitting in his recliner rocker, in his worn flannelette shirt, the newspaper in hand, and peering at me over the top of his paper. He had his old slippers on and rubbed his bald head every now and then looking quite deep in thought. He paused for ages, I was bracing myself to be told a definite 'No' but eventually, he said in his broad Scottish accent, 'I will give you my permission to do this because I know how much you love singing.' I couldn't believe my ears and set about learning my songs inside out. I never drank alcohol when I was performing because it was too important to me and more than anything in the world I wanted to be a professional singer.

The lead guitarist and another singer in the band, Bill, was keen on me. He invited me out to the movies at band practice one night. We rehearsed in his bedroom and his walls were covered with pictures of Roger Daltrey, lead singer of The Who, Led Zeppelin, and Status Quo. He was the leader of the band and Bill made the final decision about which songs we played. I didn't like him all that much at the time, as I thought he was a bit arrogant, but I agreed, and we went to see *The Devil's Playground*. The only problem was that I had to be home by eleven o'clock and the movie hadn't finished by then. So, I took off on foot, running all the way home to get in by my curfew. Bill was a bit annoyed about this, but he kept pursuing me.

Band practice was challenging sometimes. I wasn't given any say about which songs we were doing, and I was relegated to the backup singer for the first few months. We spent ages thinking of a name for the band and finally settled on 'Atlantis'. The guys wanted to do lots of 'cock rock' stuff like 'I Can't Get Enough of Your Love' by Bad Company and 'Once Bitten Twice Shy' by Ian Hunter. I disliked singing 'Junior's Farm' by Paul McCartney and 'Watch that Man' by David Bowie—both great songs, but they just didn't suit my voice. I felt very conspicuous on stage and there were not many other females in bands during the mid-seventies.

The band continued rehearsing. I think we rehearsed for about ten months before we played a gig anywhere. Our first night was at a small country hall in Laang with lots of old farmers and their wives. I was so excited to be finally performing and spent all day getting ready. Jane and I used to put water in some oatmeal and use that as a face pack, wipe it off and steam our faces over a bowl of boiling water to get rid of any blackheads.

Then I rummaged through my wardrobe and agonised over what to wear. I ended up in my only pair of Levi's, denim Jag boots, a checked shirt, and a shawl that my nanna had made me. I thought I looked pretty cool. I just found this old shawl in a bag in my garage the other day. Ahh, the memories!

We loaded up a friend's old Kingswood station wagon with all the amps and gear and set off in excited anticipation. I remember 'Hot Stuff' by the Rolling Stones blaring out of the car speakers and having butterflies in my tummy. I was so excited to finally be playing live.

We started playing, and a lady put her hands over her ears because we were so loud. Several people came up to complain and we had to tone it down a few decibels. Things loosened up later in the evening and then the power went out as we had blown all the old fuses in the hall. The State Electricity Commission was called in to fix the problem and we ended up playing until after midnight. I was sold on my new vocation as a 'rock chick' and couldn't wait until our next gig.

I did the backup vocals for a long time until I was allowed to sing 'Rhiannon' by Fleetwood Mac. The *Rumours* album had just been released and was huge in the charts. Stevie Nicks was one of my idols and I loved her 'witchy' persona and gypsy clothes. I grabbed this opportunity with both hands and learned every nuance of Stevie's raspy voice. I played the song so much that Dad threatened to throw my little yellow plastic cassette player out the window. I learned that song inside out. When I finally performed 'Rhiannon', the audiences loved it and we often had to play it a couple of times during a gig.

This led to me having other songs to do the lead vocals on such as 'I Got the Music' by Kiki Dee and 'It's So Easy' by Linda Ronstadt. I was totally in my element and I couldn't wait for each weekend to roll around so I could sing. It was strange that my anxiety seemed to disappear when I was singing. I just felt very comfortable on stage. It was my 'safe' place.

Mum and Dad allowed me to go to see Linda Ronstadt perform at the MCG in February 1979. I was so excited to be seeing my idol in real life. She came out onstage in a pair of roller skates and short shorts. The crowd went wild. I think I held my breath when she appeared on stage, and you could have heard a pin drop when she sang 'Love Me Tender' by Elvis Presley. Her voice was so strong and pure; she had perfect pitch. I was in heaven and went home more determined to be Australia's Linda.

On my sixteenth birthday, I was given the Kate Bush album *The Kick Inside* as a gift. I loved this album and played it over and over, learning it off by heart. I used to put on my silky nightie and sit beside our slow combustion stove in the kitchen singing, *'Night after night in the quiet house, plaiting her hair by the fire, woman, with no lover to ease her desire'* feeling like a heroine from a Victorian novel. Kate Bush was added to my list of idols and every time she appeared on TV in her red dress singing 'Wuthering Heights', I was captivated by her eerie dance moves and voice. One Sunday night I recall Bill's older brother, Max, sitting at the dining room table watching Kate Bush singing 'Babooshka' and dropping his soup spoon into his bowl, splashing tomato soup all over the table, when she pulled back her swords over her scantily clad thighs.

One Saturday arvo we were rehearsing in a church hall and one of the guys told me to move clockwise. I moved anticlockwise and I was mortified when he said with a snigger, 'Lucky you can sing.' I didn't realise at the time that I was brave for being a lone female in a band. I wish I could go back in time in the DeLorean from the movie *Back to the Future* and kick that guy's arse! I felt very embarrassed, and I sat on a wall outside by myself and smoked a couple of cigarettes, feeling small and stupid.

The band played a lot and gained quite a good reputation in Warrnambool. We changed the band name from Atlantis to The Detours because that was the first name the band The Who had used. Max and Bill were huge fans of The Who and we had a huge banner painted by a local sign writer that we placed behind us when we performed.

I recall playing at the Warrnambool Surf Club one night and an older woman was taking a fancy to me. I went and hid in the loo and heard the guys calling me for the next set over the PA system. They thought it was hilarious that I was being pursued by an older woman, but I was shitting myself. I knew that I certainly wasn't gay and this overt attention from another female was very disturbing to me.

I decided to walk home that night because it wasn't very far. I was halfway down Pertobe Road when Bill came limping up behind me. I turned around when I heard footsteps and Bill grabbed me in a hug and said, 'I love you.' I was quite astonished by this outburst and my teenage brain decided that I was now taken and would have to be faithful to Bill for all eternity.

25

I must mention the ABC television program *Countdown* at this point. *Countdown* was the music program that ran from 1974 until 1986 on the ABC every Sunday evening hosted by Ian 'Molly' Meldrum. It was an absolute must-watch for any self-respecting teenager, and you did not front up to school on Monday morning if you had missed it. This show gave both international acts and Australian bands huge exposure and many Aussie acts became successful because of *Countdown*. Our band supported a Sydney band called The Numbers at the Tatts Hotel in Liebig Street (now a McDonald's restaurant). The rumour was that Molly was going to come and check us out, but he never showed up. We were all very disappointed but kept hoping that our break would happen one day. We were also asked to support the band Australian Crawl while they were in town at the height of their fame one night because their support band couldn't make it. After ringing around frantically to organise everyone we were unable to do it because a couple of the guys were away on holidays.

Bill was quite hard on me while we were playing. There was never a 'Well done,' or 'God, you sang that well tonight,' after a gig. The guys would have their 'traveller' beers on the way home and argue about whose knee I would sit on. I just kept quiet and let them patronise me. I never thought to challenge them or say, 'Hey, I will sit where I bloody well like after lugging the gear and singing my guts out all night!' Even though their attitudes were quite sexist, I was never exempt from carting the gear, even the heavy PA speakers and amps.

The novel *Puberty Blues*, by Kathy Lette and Gabrielle Carey, hit the nail on the head regarding what society was like for adolescent girls in the 1970s in Australia. I remember reading it and thinking, *Spot on!* We were just for decoration. Girls didn't have a voice and if you did speak up you were a 'bloody feminist' or an ugly moll. At gigs, girls would avoid me like the plague and I overheard a conversation in the loo once where one girl said to another, 'I bet she sleeps with all of them.' As if the only reason I was in the band was to give sexual favours to the guys. I was gobsmacked even then.

The guys in the band surfed as well, and I was the snack bearer and gear minder a lot. 'I'll have a pie with sauce and a can of Coke,' was the standard order. My friends were astonished that I got to hang around with the 'cool guys'. This gave me status at school because these guys were 'very cool'. I rarely said anything when I was with them though because I thought I was inferior. I would just sing my backup vocals, look good doing it, and tolerate their blatant chauvinism.

I enjoyed dressing up when I was performing and spent a lot of time reading my *Dolly* magazines for ideas and visiting the op shops in town looking for interesting clothes. Dad was a very frugal man, and he didn't like to spend any money on unnecessary items, such as fancy clothes. I was a creative girl and I spent a lot of time making my clothes on Mum's old Singer sewing machine. I would buy old dresses and use the lovely vintage fabrics to make new outfits. I wore many of these creations while I was performing, and I was often asked where I bought my clothes. I enjoyed designing these outfits so much that I considered studying fashion design at the Gordon Institute of Technology in Geelong. Nanna caught wind of this and wasn't pleased about it. I can remember her saying, 'I know that you like sewing and fashion but there isn't much future in that line of work.' I felt disappointed, but I knew better than to argue with the family matriarch. She said that I was a clever girl and that I would be much better off studying to be a teacher. I was sad about this because I loved designing new outfits and I had a passion for fashion.

The band played in some very odd locations like shearing sheds, country halls, and people's parties. I recall one gig where the patrons kept asking us to play country and western songs. We quickly worked out the chords to *Stand by Your Man* and played it about five times!

It was a scene very reminiscent of the movie *The Blues Brothers* when they played a country and western bar behind chicken wire and got pelted with bottles.

I remember playing at a dimly lit venue one night and there was a guy in a suit leaning against a wall watching us play all night. At the end of the gig, he came over and spoke to me. I thought he was just going to try to chat me up. He said, 'You have a lot of talent and I reckon you could go places, but lose the guy up the front with you.' Bill wanted to know what the guy had said, and I told him. It was a quiet trip home that night and, as far as Bill was concerned, we were a double act and there was no way I would have been able to strike out on my own.

In a future band, this was once again brought to my attention. Our lead guitarist, who was a very talented muso, asked me to come over one Saturday morning for a cuppa. I liked this guy and we got on well. He looked out for me when some of the 'punters' got a bit too friendly, and we shared jokes and had a similar outlook on life. When I arrived at his place that Saturday morning, he looked a bit sheepish. I asked, 'What's up?' to which he replied, 'I have been thinking about this a lot and I really can't continue to play in the band.' I was quite dumbfounded and confused by this as we sounded great. I was worried that he was going to say, 'Your singing is ordinary' or 'You aren't good enough.' He looked at me and said, 'I just can't stand the way Bill treats you and puts you down all the time. You are a very talented singer and I can't stand by and watch it anymore, so I am going to have to leave the band.'

I was shocked really, and it made a big impact on me that someone had recognised what was happening in my life and then had the guts to tell me.

Chapter 4
School and smokes

One Monday morning after I had dragged my sorry arse out of bed and made myself get on the school bus, our Year Ten form teacher introduced a new student. She was from Melbourne; her dad was a cop and had been transferred to a country position. She was pretty, with blonde hair and blue eyes, and I decided right then that she would become my new best friend.

As I was class captain, I was asked to show her around and take her under my wing. I did so gladly, and we did become great friends. Sally and I sat together on the bus as she lived in the next suburb from me. We smoked cigarettes, shared our snacks, and hung around together. I was so rapt to finally have a friend of my own. Her home life wasn't great, though, and her dad was prone to drinking a bit and getting quite aggressive. She was unhappy a lot of the time, and I tried to be a supportive listener.

Bill and I started going out together as a couple not long after Elvis died in 1977; I can remember talking to him about it. We virtually became inseparable, sitting together at recess and lunchtime every day at school and talking on the phone every night, until Dad yelled, 'Get off the phone!'

I can still remember sitting in the unheated passage where the old, yellow, rotary phone was placed on our very seventies telephone table and twisting the yellow phone cord around my fingers. Bill rang me every weeknight at seven o'clock. It was freezing in winter and I used to grab my wonky purple crochet blanket to put over my knees.

I saw a lot of Bill and I came to know his family quite well, as we rehearsed at his place two nights a week and some weekends. I used to save my lunch money at school so Bill and I could go and check out bands at the pubs around town on the weekends we weren't playing ourselves. I recall my tummy rumbling in class because I would only eat an apple all day. Meanwhile, Bill would be munching into his sausage rolls, pies, and Twisties every recess and lunchtime. He rarely offered me a bite or even one Twistie, so I just chewed my apple slowly. I was thin and hungry most of the time.

Bill's mum, Berryl, would make us sandwiches. I remember the first time I had lunch at his place: Bill's dad, Bob, said to me, 'Pass us the dead horse for me maggoty eye.' I had no idea what he was talking about, and they were all laughing. It was Australian slang for, 'Pass me the tomato sauce for my pie.' I realised at that point that Bill and I were from very different backgrounds. I don't think my upbringing would've been much different if I had been raised in Scotland. Bill's family were very Australian and quite reserved; no-one said much around the table, and you did not talk about your feelings or anything emotional.

A couple of years earlier, Bill had been in a serious accident while riding his bike home from school. He had been in hospital for quite a long time in Melbourne after breaking his back and smashing his ankle. This accident had left him with several health issues, and he continued to have operations to fuse his ankle and improve his mobility.

The accident had also affected his sexual function and we didn't begin an intimate relationship because of this for a couple of years. I went to the doctor by myself at seventeen and got a script for the contraceptive pill. This certainly ruled out becoming pregnant, but I was always frustrated by the brevity of our encounters. I was a passionate young lass, and this caused me to 'turn off' to save myself from constant disappointment. I can recall putting on Mum's lipstick and styling a sheet over my shoulder and pretending to be Venus the goddess of love, holding up Mum's brush as my torch. Looking back I feel sad for that young girl who started drinking more to deal with her unmet needs and missed out on a wonderful part of life.

Bill had one sibling, an older brother called Max, who played bass guitar in the band. They tended to fight a lot and I felt like the referee a lot of the time. It made rehearsals awkward and only added to my anxiety about not being good enough. Max stood behind me on stage when we were performing, and I always felt like his eyes were boring through my back. I couldn't relax and enjoy the experience. Our lead guitarist, Fred, was a good friend of Max and he always looked out for me and gave me a confident nod when I needed it. He nicknamed me 'Magenta' because we played a couple of songs from *The Rocky Horror Show* and Magenta is one of the lead characters.

I went on holidays with Bill and his family in their caravan. We had some great times and I enjoyed camping with them in seaside caravan parks. Every Christmas school holidays, the van went down the beach to number one caravan park in Warrnambool and we enjoyed being tourists at home. I got to sleep in the annexe and many days and nights were spent at the beach, jumping up and down on the beachside trampolines to 'Living in the '70s' by Skyhooks, playing totem tennis, sunbathing, and going to the surf club disco.

I remember one evening playing backgammon with Bill in the van before bed. Bill's dad had just come back from the loo and I had my skimpy red shorty pyjamas on. His eyes nearly popped out of his head as I recall, but I had no idea why. He mumbled something to Bill and went up the end of the van to bed. He never acted inappropriately with me at all, quite the opposite. I had a good relationship with both Bill's parents, and they treated me like the daughter they never had.

I liked listening to Led Zeppelin and fooling around in the van when Bill's folks were out. I loved snuggling up and being affectionate which often became quite heated. It was always a frustrating experience though for me. Even today, when I hear *'Whole Lotta Love'* by Led Zeppelin, I get a sinking feeling in the pit of my stomach. It never occurred to me to end the relationship if I was unhappy. I was very committed because of our musical connection, I suppose and felt that it would mean the band's end if we broke up. I was so distraught about this that I did speak to our drummer about it one night. Of course, this got back to Bill, and he was not impressed with me at all. Things were quite fragile for a while after this but eventually, Bill forgave me.

In 1978, a group of students from high school went on the annual snow trip to Falls Creek in Victoria. The principal called Bill and me into his office and told us that we could not spend any time alone together on this trip. I was a bit miffed about this, but Bill went off with his mates and I hardly saw him. I remember sitting on the bus by myself feeling sad and listening to 'Baker Street' by Gerry Rafferty, while Bill was laughing and fooling around up the back of the bus with his mates.

On the first night in Melbourne, a group of girls met up in someone's room. One of the girls got out a bottle of grog and some smokes. There were about six of us, I think. We were chatting, giggling, and smoking away when there was a knock at the door.

'Shit, teachers; get in the wardrobe,' someone said. Another girl and I dived into the wardrobe, crushing out our fags on the way. The teachers caught two of the girls and they got sent home straight away. No-one said anything about me and the other lass who had hidden in the wardrobe. We continued the trip in absolute fear that someone would dob us in and we would get sent home too.

It wasn't until the following week back at school that I heard my name called out over the PA system. 'Would Margaret Jackson come to the principal's office immediately?' I was terrified! I walked up to his office with my legs shaking, feeling like I was about to throw up. I put my hands on my legs, willing them to stop shaking while I was waiting on the bench outside. He ushered me into his office and sat down, putting his elbows on his desk, fingertips steepled together.

He looked at me very sternly, peering at me over the specs on his nose, and said, 'Were you hiding in the wardrobe after smoking and drinking with several girls at The People's Palace in Melbourne last week?'

I could hardly breathe but managed to croak out, 'Yes, sir, I was.'

He gave me a good dressing-down, saying that it was a very deceitful thing to do when others had been sent home, and that he would have to punish me appropriately. He certainly did that. The band was playing at the end-of-term social the following week and he suspended me from school for two days, which included the night of the social. Bill had to do all the vocals and I was at home, grounded and sulking in my bedroom. Needless to say, I wasn't very popular at home either, so it was a big lesson in owning up to my mistakes.

Jane used to worry about me a lot. Sharing a bedroom, I naturally spent more time with her than anyone else. She wasn't all that keen on Bill and one day they argued about something, and she told him that he wasn't a nice person. She said years later that it had turned her off from having a boyfriend because he wasn't nice to me.

When I was learning to drive, he said that I would never be able to drive a manual car and to just get my automatic licence because that would be easier. I thought, *No way; I am getting my manual licence.* I had lessons with a driving school and I worked hard to become a good driver. One day, Bill took me out for a practice, and we weren't far from my house when he said, 'Shit, if there was a pothole you would hit it.' I was cross. I pulled the car over, told him to get stuffed, slammed the car door, and walked home.

He did enjoy putting people down and feeling superior to them. Elizabeth used to say that he was arrogant. I was aware of this, and we argued quite a lot, but I was so trapped in my unworthiness that I rarely disagreed or challenged him. I thought I deserved to be treated poorly.

Life continued on with me playing in the band at weekends, sewing new and unique outfits for my rock-chick image, and studying hard at school to get top marks. I can remember our high school friends chartering a bus to come and see the band play in a country hall somewhere. I was friendly with a lot of the people in Bill's year, especially a girl called Sandy. She would always take the time to chat with me at school and I felt a special bond with her. We hung around in the same social group and had a lot of friends in common. I introduced her to Sally at school one day and the three of us became firm friends.

I decided that I would attend the Warrnambool Institute of Advanced Education, or Deakin University, as it is called now, to study primary teaching. Sandy had gone to study in Melbourne after she finished her HSC and wasn't happy in the city, so she returned to Warrnambool after only one year there. Sandy and Sally asked me what I intended to study, and I told them I was going to train to be a teacher, so they enrolled in the same course and we became a very tight trio. Bill had taken a gap year after his HSC and then started his training to be a nurse. This appealed to him greatly after he had been looked after so well by the nursing staff in the hospital in Melbourne following his accident. We were both able to live at home while we studied, which appealed to us at the time as well.

Bill purchased a campervan with the insurance money that he received from his accident, and we spent many weekends down the Great Ocean Road camping with our crazy labrador pup, Hymie. The band was still going strong, too, although we had a new drummer, my cousin, and a new lead guitarist by this time.

Sandy and Sally liked to party and go to barrels that were held on campus. I used to go with them if I had completed enough study.

They used to joke when someone asked where I was when they were smoking and drinking coffee in the student cafe, by pointing upwards with a pious expression on their faces. That meant I was in the library above the café, studying. They both thought that I was a 'conch' and used to tease me about it. I was still afraid of failure, and I strove hard to get top marks in all my subjects. My besties weren't as studious as me and made the most of the student entertainment. They always came to our gigs and their favourite song was 'So Lonely' by The Police.

We all smoked liked chimneys and even used to sit in Sandy's car in the Deakin carpark before lectures having a joint before class. Our favourite lecturer was Paul Jennings, who was passionate about literacy and making sure that students had interesting books to read. I can recall him saying, 'Every student requires books that cultivates their love of reading at the correct level of instruction, or readability level.' I remember him stopping, whiteboard marker poised in mid-air with a wistful expression on his face.

I piped up and said, '*You* should write some kids' books, Paul,' and the lecture theatre erupted in laughter. He went on to write *Unreal* in 1985 and many other children's books that promoted children's love for literature. I was rapt that Paul had pursued a successful writing career, and I used his fantastic books in my classrooms for my whole teaching career.

Every Wednesday, Friday, and Sunday night, we would head to the Criterion Hotel, known as the wildest pub in town, to drink cask moselle by the gallon, then we graduated to riesling for a while, before going more up market to the 'chardonnay club' and we finally finished our wine education with sauvignon blanc. I would usually have something strong to start the night off and I liked Black Russians. They were a fierce brew of vodka and Kahlua over ice. I would have one of these to start the night and I could feel the alcohol seeping into my bloodstream after the first few slugs. I could feel my body starting to relax and my awful anxiety would disappear.

Sandy had a beaten-up car called 'Scattley' and we would smuggle our friends into the drive-in theatre in the boot of her car. Her parents managed the drive-in theatre in town, and we rocked up quite a lot with boot-loads of our mates. I have wonderful memories of playing 'truth or dare' after drinking copious amounts of cask wine, while we were camping in the summer holidays at number one caravan park. We were quite buxom young lasses and we had lots of male admirers. I remember almost choking with laughter after daring the girls to do a lap of the park topless after they chose 'dare'. They stripped off, looked out of the tent flap tentatively, and took off like Cathy Freeman. I thought to myself, *If you can't beat em, join em*, and the three of us ran shrieking like banshees around the park.

On a teaching round in our first year of study, Sally and I rocked up one day wearing fairly sheer 'hippie' cheesecloth dresses with bells and mirrors on them. The infant mistress was *not amused* as the school was quite traditional and she called us into her office. 'Girls, you are both wonderful, young student teachers, but your clothing is not appropriate for the classroom'. Sally and I went to my place after school and dug out my high-collared lace shirts, long skirts, and two shawls. We went next door to ask Nanna if we could borrow her cameo brooches. The next day we went to school looking like extras from *Picnic at Hanging Rock*. The old bat passed us in the main corridor and stopped to say, 'That is much more suitable attire today, ladies.' We went to the staff room laughing our heads off, grabbed a coffee each, and lit up a smoke.

Bill and I took a trip to Fiji at the end of 1981. While we were there, Bill went up to the house band and asked them if his girlfriend could sing with them. I was quite reluctant, to be honest, as I was there for a holiday, not to perform. He was very persistent as always and I got up and did 'Blue Bayou' à la Linda Ronstadt. I even had the flower behind my ear, long dark hair, and I had been told that I resembled her. The next morning, a big basket of fruit arrived at our room with an invitation to join the band at rehearsal that afternoon. I thought it was quite funny and I went to the rehearsal. The band were all acting strangely and kowtowing to me. Finally, the penny dropped, and I realised that they thought I was Linda herself on holidays! It took me a while to explain that Linda is an American and I am Australian. I was very flattered to be mistaken for my idol and the following night at the bar it was packed, you could not move! I was offered a three-month season to sing with the band and rang Dad in Australia to ask him. He said, 'You have to come home and finish your teacher training first before running off to join a band.' How different my life might have turned out if I had stayed and sung in Fiji. This was a 'sliding doors' moment.

One tropical night, strolling along the beach in Mana Island Fiji, Bill turned and said, 'I think we should get married when we go home.' I was all loved-up and on holidays, so I said, 'Yes'. We looked at engagement rings in Nandi but we were a bit broke at the time. We waited until we went home to Australia, and Bill surprised me in May 1982 with a sparkling, solitaire diamond engagement ring while we were out for dinner to celebrate my nineteenth birthday. The family were a bit surprised but gave us their blessing and we started organising our wedding for the following year.

We started looking at houses to buy early in 1983. We went to view quite a few of them, but I wasn't keen on most of the places. The real estate agent that we had been dealing with called us on the morning of our hens' and bucks' night to tell us that this place had just gone on the market and to come and look at it straight away. We drove around to the address he had given us, and both said, 'This can't be it, surely—not for forty grand.' We liked it straight away. An old couple owned the place, and she was baking scones, so the place smelt delicious and was so homey. The decor was awful! There were cream carpets with brown swirls (we used to call it the shit-brown carpet), *bright* yellow bench tops, daisy wallpaper, and purple shag pile carpet in the ensuite bathroom. We could see that it had a lot of potential though, a great location, sea views and the place just had a great 'vibe'. We didn't even really discuss it, just got to the front porch after looking through it and said, 'We'll take it!'

I remember that night vividly. Sally's mum, Elaine, held a hens' party for me at her place and we played lots of drinking games. I had lost so much weight that the bubbly went straight to my head and I was violently ill. Sally, Sandy, and Jane had to put me in the shower to clean me up and they were shocked when they saw my bones poking out of my emaciated frame. I had definitely developed an eating disorder on top of my depression and anxiety.

Chapter 5
Getting married

Looking out the bridal car window on the way to the church on August 20, 1983, I wanted Dad to give me some good advice or reassure me that I was making the right decision. I was twenty years old, in my final year of my teacher training, and about to marry my high school sweetheart.

Dad and I sat in silence on our way to the wedding and, strangely, I recall this so vividly above other memories of that day. When we alighted from the car, there is a photo of me beaming and Dad looking every inch the proud father. I look at that pic and wonder what he was thinking at the time. It was the only wedding that I have ever been to where we had to wait until it stopped pouring rain to leave the church. I left with a friend of Bill's jacket over my head, so I wouldn't ruin my hairdo or get soaked.

It was a brilliant wedding. Dad, Jane, and Allan all sang at the church. Jane, Sandy, and Sally were my bridesmaids. Sally hated her pink chiffon bridesmaids' dress and said, 'Shit, Margy, this frock makes me look like one of the elephants in that Disney animation, *Fantasia*.' All the Australian-based relatives were there, and the Scottish ones all sent telegrams. At the wedding reception at our local golf club, our master of ceremonies was a man called Barney Miller who had travelled on the ship to Australia with Mum and her family in 1955. Barney and his family had remained life-long friends of my grandparents and had been to visit many times. He had a wonderful sense of humour and had everyone in fits of laughter. In his speech, Barney said, 'Like a butterfly emerges and unfolds its graceful wings, a marriage grows, and it develops with the love each partner brings.'

There wasn't a dry eye in the room when Barney had finished his speech. My dad followed this up by saying, 'With their mutual love of music, I hope they will stay in step and be a good team.' That was right before he came up to me in a panic, saying, 'It is only nine o'clock and the bar tab has been spent already.' Luckily, Bob passed the hat around and put quite a lot more money on the bar.

The whole band was at the reception and we got up in our wedding gear and blew the roof off the place. Our friends commented to us for months afterwards that it was the best wedding they had ever attended. They all said that it was 'cool as' seeing a bride rock out to 'Rock and Roll' by Led Zeppelin. I can recall how strange it felt grooving onstage with my big, hooped skirt and I kept snagging my veil on the mic stand. Pat Benatar's song 'Hit Me with Your Best Shot' was popular at the time and Sally said that it was funny seeing a bride boxing and jumping around on stage. The guys were all in tuxedos and there is a brilliant photo of Bill holding up his guitar in the air triumphantly with his tuxedo tails flying.

Sally and Sandy were a bit upset when I dedicated the song 'So Lonely' by The Police to the bridesmaids. It *was* their favourite song at the time, so I wasn't being spiteful. I can still see the image of them dancing together, crying and slow dancing in their unpopular pink chiffon creations while I was singing the song.

After Bill's mate drove us back to our motel for the night and smoked several joints with Bill (I had fallen asleep by then), we got up early and Max and my new sister-in-law, Aggie, drove us to Melbourne. I recall sitting at Tullamarine Airport with a cup of coffee, feeling exhausted. We boarded our flight to Kuala Lumpur and stayed there in a hotel overnight. I recall a uniformed maid wheeling in a trolley with silver cloches on it the following morning and thinking, *Our first meal together as husband and wife*, shortly followed by, *I don't think we will be having too many fancy breakfasts like this.*

We continued to Club Med Cherating Beach for the first week of our honeymoon. We met several other Aussies and claimed our table near the bar for the next week. We all drank for Australia, and we didn't let the team down. I had starved myself to look good in my wedding dress; I weighed forty-six kilos the day I got married. I recall Sandy and Sally saying, 'You are getting thinner and thinner and browner and browner.' Solariums were all the rage in 1983 and I wanted to look slim and tanned in my wedding dress. My wedding dress had to be taken in three times before the wedding day. This was very tedious because there were about fifty pearl buttons down the back of the dress that had to be removed and resewn each time. I was fixated on being as thin as possible to look good in my dress and starved myself for weeks on end. So, I let loose and had a good time on our honeymoon, eating and drinking everything in sight.

The resort was tropical and lush. There were lots of young Australian couples and we would meet up around the pool and have drinks and swim. Every day there was a buffet of all you could eat for breakfast, lunch, and dinner. I certainly made the most of it after dieting for months on end. A little Malaysian guy had a noodle trolley that he wheeled around every afternoon at four o'clock, and I had a good go at that too. One night there was a Michael Jackson-themed disco being held at the resort night club and I wanted to go. You had to dress up and wear a glove or a pair of white socks and I thought it would be fun to go and have a dance. Bill said, 'Michael Jackson is a dickhead and I wouldn't dance to his crap if you paid me.' I felt disappointed and sat in our room feeling hard done by. I wanted to go and dance and have some fun instead of just drinking and holding up the bar every night. I could hear the faint strains of 'Billie Jean' and laughter outside the window of our room and I hoped that this wasn't the taste of what my future life was to become.

Once in Hong Kong, we were upgraded to a flasher hotel right beside the harbour: The Harbour View, of course! We would sit in our room and watch the junk boats sail past. I loved the vibrancy, sights, sounds, and smells of this strange place. Dad had been stationed in Hong Kong when he did his Scottish national service in the early fifties, so I had heard heaps of stories about what a fascinating place it was. Dad used to say, 'I had the best tomato soup I have ever tasted in Hong Kong.' I spent a lot of time walking around the streets of Hong Kong exploring the city while Bill stayed at the hotel drinking our duty-free grog or recovering from a drinking binge. I don't have one memory of us walking around hand in hand in typical honeymoon style or sharing any romantic moments on this trip. I tried to be positive and hoped that things would improve when we got home and into our own place.

I remember Jane surprising us by turning up at Spencer Street Station when we arrived back in Melbourne from our honeymoon. She was studying at Melbourne Uni and popped down on a tram to welcome us home. I was so pleased to see my little sister and hugged her tightly before jumping on the six o'clock train back home to Warrnambool.

We rented a one-bedroom flat just across the road from the Warrnambool Base Hospital where Bill was nursing. The flat was forty-five bucks a week including electricity, and I was so happy to be living in our own place. We had already bought our house before the wedding and only had to rent until the ninety-day settlement was up. In these first three months together as newlyweds, we got into the habit of having a wine or three with our evening meal. We felt very 'grown up' drinking from our fancy new wine glasses and having our friends over for dinner. I recall turning on the radio one morning in September 1983 and hearing Bob Hawke, who was our prime minister back then, saying, 'Any boss who sacks anyone for not turning up today is a bum,' after Australia had won the America's Cup. I walked past that flat the other day and a memory of us snuggled up in bed popped into my mind. I was really 'up for it' but Bill said, 'I'm tired and I have to get up early and go to work tomorrow.' I felt sad and rejected a lot of the time. I thought it was usually the woman who said, 'I've got a headache'? Bill just didn't understand physical or emotional intimacy and at twenty years old, I was unsure how to address it.

Moving into our own house in our hometown of Warrnambool the week before Christmas in 1983 was nothing short of fantastic. I recall saying to Bill, 'Christmas might be a bit meagre this year as we only have twenty dollars left in the bank.'

Bill still had ten thousand dollars left from his accident compensation and we had used this as the deposit on our house. The bank was quite reticent to lend us the thirty thousand dollars home loan we applied for because I had just finished studying and didn't have a job. Bob and Berryl came in to bat for us because Bob played golf with the bank manager, and we received our thirty-thousand-dollar home loan. It is quite staggering to think that our first home cost forty thousand dollars in 1983, complete with sea views, a garage, two bathrooms, and three bedrooms, in the very tightly held area of East Warrnambool.

It was great having our own place and our friends loved coming around to visit. One evening in January 1984, I had invited Sandy and Sally around for a video night. Sandy turned up with the Coolabah cask of moselle and we had a couple of drinks while waiting for Sally to show up. When she didn't arrive, Sandy and I started to get worried. Our home phone rang, and it was Sally's mum, Elaine, sounding very distressed. 'Margy, Sally has been in a serious accident involving her bike and a ute … and … *sob … ooh God … sob …* I am up at the emergency department at the base.' We jumped into my car straight away and headed up to the hospital. Sally rode a motorbike and while riding that day, just out of town, a farmer had pulled out of his driveway suddenly and collected her while she was riding past. Her left leg had been pinned under her bike and she was in a bad way. We stayed at the hospital until the nurses let us in to see her and prayed that she would be okay.

The next twelve months passed in a flurry of stripping old wallpaper off walls, sanding back doors and architraves, pulling lots of old plastic out of piles of dirt in the back yard, and trying to improve our home. I didn't start teaching straight away because jobs were quite scarce, so I did some home tutoring and emergency relief teaching. Bill scored a nursing job at an old folks' home near our house and I tried to become Mrs. Perfect Housewife. I think I had watched too many episodes of *Bewitched* and *The Brady Bunch* as a child and I was trying to emulate what I believed the *perfect* housewife should be.

I look back on this as my 'Doris Day' period and I even had a bobbed hairdo and wore crisply pressed shirts and neat pants to complete my transition to a married lady. I certainly was good at morphing into whatever role I was playing in my life at any given time. (I always thought I could give Nicole Kidman a run for her money.) It was a strange year because I had finished studying, I was married, I owned a house, and I was only twenty years old.

Sally was hospitalised for months as her left leg wasn't healing very well. I visited her most days in the hospital and tried to cheer her up. She was very depressed and started drinking heavily to numb the pain and her disappointment at the length of time she had to remain in hospital. Every time I went to visit her, she had a bottle of Jack Daniels and a glass beside her on the table. It was our twenty-first birthdays that May, so I organised a surprise party at my place. Sandy was able to get permission for Sally to leave the hospital for one day and we all hid inside my house waiting to surprise her. A male friend carried her up the front steps, opened my front door and we all called out *'Surprise!'* It was a terrific celebration. We drank heaps of wine and presented Sally with a cane peacock chair, a huge pink bow on top, for her birthday present. She loved it and Bill took a photo of the three of us toasting our birthdays after Sally received her special present.

I have always enjoyed cooking and I strove to create yummy meals for us to eat. I was particularly proud of a dish that I had made one evening and Bill said, 'Nearly as good as Mum's.' Berryl was a fantastic cook and had set the bar very high. She was prone to 'popping in' with advice and to lend a hand. I was totally mortified when she came one morning to help me make our bed, offering to help me change the sheets!

Berryl had definitely spoilt Bill, picking up after him and attending to his every whim. I was expected to continue in her footsteps. That caused quite a few arguments to say the least. She was quite flabbergasted with me once and said, 'Do you know what your problem is, Margy?' I shook my head to say no. 'You wear your heart on your sleeve.' I thought this was a compliment and I was quite chuffed about it.

I coped with doing all the domestic tasks when I was a stay-at-home housewife but this changed when I received a telegram in February 1985 to say that I had been offered a full-time teaching position at a school seventy kilometres away, in Cobden.

Chapter 6
Teaching

Driving up the potholed and oh-so-familiar road to my first teaching post, I lit yet another cigarette. I was toying with the idea of just having a 'little accident', enough to warrant a couple of weeks of rest at home. I was stressed out of my brain, totally overwhelmed with the responsibility of educating twenty-seven little minds, and the one-hundred-and-forty-kilometre round trip every day was exhausting.

My year one and two composite class were a nice bunch of kids, and I worked as hard as I could to be a competent teacher. Being in total control of your own class was different from being on teaching rounds. I found the responsibility overwhelming, and I worried that I wasn't doing a good enough job. Term one 1985 was fifteen weeks and four days long. We had booked a trip to Bali for the May school holidays and I felt like I was crawling on my hands and knees over broken glass to get to the last day of term.

Cobden in southwest Victoria had a large population of Jehovah's Witnesses in 1985 and I had seven of these students in my class. I found it very difficult to provide teaching activities that didn't include Easter, fairies, witches, birthdays, Hallowe'en, or Christmas. It was a tough year and I got into trouble more than once allowing these kids to listen to a 'forbidden story' or select a special treat from the 'clever' box.

The vice-principal's son was also in my class, which added even more pressure to my already frayed nerves. I would wake up each school morning with my stomach in knots, smoke a couple of cigarettes before I left for school, go to the loo with the runs, then smoke all the way to school, mentally counting down how many days of term were left in my head.

I didn't select the best profession for a person who struggles with anxiety and depression. Teaching is the type of job that can 'suck you dry' if you are prone to giving a lot of yourself. I gave it everything I had and more that year and Bill got very tired of listening to my blow-by-blow account of what happened each day. My drinking to self-medicate increased and so did my anxiety. I developed awful blisters on my hands and had to wear hand cream and a pair of cotton gloves to bed every night. I went to see a doctor in Cobden about this. She asked me about my anxiety and stress, and I downplayed it because she was a parent of one of my students. I continued on, but I know that I struggled through that year. I was once again euphoric driving home from school on Friday nights listening to 'Everybody Wants to Rule the World' by Tears for Fears. We would go out to our favourite pizza restaurant, Bojangles, for dinner and drink heaps of wine. Saturday I would scrub the house from top to bottom mildly hungover and then often play a gig. We had formed a new band, called The Twisters, after our high school band had fizzled out with only Bill and me as original members. On Sunday, I would start to realise that another week of misery was about to start and take to the couch and mope.

Sally's leg had not healed, even after several skin grafts and a stint in a rehabilitation hospital in Melbourne. We were shocked when she called to say that her leg was going to be amputated because gangrene had set into the wound and caused further complications. It was a stressful time and Sandy and I felt extremely anxious about Sally's mental state as she was very depressed and low. Her operation to remove the leg was in July 1985 and Sally remained in Melbourne to recover from the amputation, arriving back home in September to be cared for by her lovely mum Elaine.

I rang the District Inspector of Education in December 1985 and said, 'I would like a teaching transfer back to Warrnambool or I will resign from the Education Department.' I knew that I couldn't do another year at Cobden because my anxiety was extreme, and I just wasn't coping well at school. This man was an acquaintance of my dad because he was Scottish, and he had been the Inspector of Schools when I was a pupil myself. My first-grade teacher, Mrs. Fitzgerald, always asked me to read aloud when he visited because I was a good reader, and it must've scored her points on her performance review. The next day, he got back to me and told me that there was a 'shared specialist' position available for the following year and to get my application in straight away. I got the job teaching music and drama at Merrivale, Dennington, South Warrnambool, and Allansford primary schools, spending one day in each school and rotating around each school on Fridays.

I was in my element in this position. It allowed me to pursue my love of music and performing and give kids the opportunity to develop their skills. A former student recently told me that the kids would wait outside near the carpark on the day I was coming and race each other to my car (a Triumph TR7) to be first, so they could carry my guitar and percussion instruments into the school. I formed a combined choir with about twenty-five kids from each school and we were rapt when we won the primary choral section at the local Eisteddfod in 1986. The song we sang was 'Flashdance ... What a Feeling' in three parts, and the kids had rehearsed for months to receive the highest score possible from the adjudicators. When they were announced as winners all the kids jumped out of their seats cheering. I was so thrilled about this because they were students from smaller schools, and they had never performed on a professional stage in a theatre before. I felt elated that I was able to give my students this experience.

Bill had gone away to train as a psychiatric nurse when I started writing a musical for kids in 1987. I was in the staffroom at Allansford Primary School one day telling a colleague that a sweet student had given me a card saying, 'You are my superhero'. I remember saying, 'I've got a great idea, let's do a combined musical called "Superheroes".'

Everyone looked at me like I was bonkers, but they all climbed onboard and what a hectic, exhilarating, and challenging year it was. It was a huge project working with four different schools and over one hundred students. I undertook writing a script about a group of superheroes who visit a school and recruit the students to make the world a kinder place. I also wrote the songs and coordinated getting everyone together in the same place for rehearsals. I would teach all day and then come home, wine glass beside my pad and write, sometimes into the wee small hours.

At times I felt like the play was writing itself, my creative juices were flowing easily. I carried a pen and pad around with me everywhere that year, so I could write down any ideas if they popped into my head.

I was asked to go to Somers Camp with the students from my schools in September 1987. It was a ten-day camp at Somers in Gippsland, run by the education department, which is still provided for students in Years Five and Six from all locations in Victoria every two years. It was Barwon South Western's turn that year and I was looking forward to having a break from the musical and doing something different. The student who played the lead female role in *Superheroes* was on this camp and we met several times to go over her lines for the show. One day, she was engrossed in a book when I went to find her. I said, 'What are you reading, sweetheart?' She showed me the cover and it was *Unreal* by Paul Jennings. She said, 'This is a fantastic book, you should read it.' I laughed out loud, thinking to myself, *Paul did write his book* and I did read it on that trip.

I met a fellow teacher called Tom on this camp and we hit it off immediately. He was funny and charming and extremely handsome. Nothing untoward happened on this trip but I knew that he liked me and I thought he was very attractive. We caught up for a drink when the camp was over, but he was married with two small children and we didn't see each other again for many years.

As busy as I was teaching and writing the musical, I was also very lonely. I wasn't used to living by myself and I started drinking quite a lot to self-soothe. Bill would ring in the evenings but there was no, 'Hi, I really miss you,' or any loving chitchat. I was an aerobics freak and went about four times a week in my typical eighties fluoro Lycra G-string leotard and leg warmers. The Twisters played nearly every weekend and we hardly had any time to see one another. Setting up at a pub on Valentine's Day 1987 a guy across the bar said to his mates, 'Look, there she is: the girl I am going to marry.' I laughed, thinking this was funny, but he came to every gig we played at.

I told him that I was married to the rhythm guitarist but that didn't deter him. I liked this guy as he was very good-looking and had a great smile. I got to know him quite well after speaking with him at lots of gigs and he started phoning me. Things between Bill and me were not good at this point. Bill had made new friends doing his training and didn't seem overly happy to come home at weekends. I would wait at the picture window in our kitchen, looking forward to seeing him every Friday night, sitting there in my cane wicker chair, wine glass and cigarette in hand, watching for his car lights to appear in our driveway. He would walk up the front stairs and just say, 'G'day how are ya?'

I would reply, 'I am okay, but I feel really lonely.' Then he would just go and get a beer from the fridge. There was no big hug or any show of affection. I was disappointed by this and I felt really excluded and very alone for the first time in my life.

I felt very conflicted about talking to this single man and I recalled our pompous wedding minister saying, 'Don't think because you are married that you will never be attracted to anyone ever again.' I invited my suitor around for dinner one night and I was very nervous about it. It just wasn't me to be so sneaky and unfaithful. I genuinely loved Bill and I just couldn't break my wedding vows, so I refused his advances. He came around one afternoon when I had just arrived home from school and said very abruptly, 'I can't do this,' and quickly left. I felt sad and so wretched—'vexed', as my nanna would say. I have thought about this many times over the years and I do regret not experiencing a night of passion with him. I wonder if he is still single?

In December 1987, I was delighted that the four performances of *Superheroes* was sold out. Walking out from backstage at the Warrnambool Entertainment Centre after the final performance, a lady in tears grabbed me and started hugging me, saying it was the best show she had ever seen. She was only in Warrnambool on holidays and saw the *Superheroes* banner out the front and decided to buy a ticket. I was blown away by the cards, letters, and messages I received.

I started to feel very unwell a couple of days later, walking a group of students back to school after a Christmas treat of the movies. My legs were wobbling like jelly and I felt like I was going to pass out. I made it to my mum's couch because I was at South Warrnambool Primary that day and lay there before being taken to the doc with total exhaustion. I spent the majority of that summer holiday in bed resting. This had scared me a bit and I decided to give up the grog and smokes and take some 'time out' for myself for a while.

I realised I needed to be careful. I decided to pace myself better and not go at full speed all the time. Bill came home from his placement and got a job at the psychiatric hospital in town and life settled down again. I wanted our marriage to work and tried hard to communicate my needs more clearly and to be a supportive wife. We started talking about taking a trip over to the UK and spent months planning it. My Scottish cousin had invited us to her wedding in Kirkcaldy, Fife, in July 1988 and I wrote to her saying that we would love to come.

Chapter 7
Hame tae bonnie Scotland

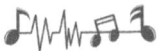

Mum and Dad saw us off at the Warrnambool railway station in July 1988. I was so excited to be returning to Scotland after thirteen years and introducing Bill to my Scottish relatives. I had taken three months' leave without pay from school and we intended to do a Contiki tour and some backpacking around Europe during our trip.

We did the 'milk run' flying all over the place on Garuda Airlines and landing in London about thirty-eight hours later. We were exhausted, and I think we were the last people to get off the plane. My uncle picked us up from Gatwick Airport and we drove to his place in Wheatley, a quaint little village outside Oxford. We had afternoon tea with my aunty and cousins and my uncle piped up and said, 'I know that we were going to set off for Scotland tomorrow morning, but I think it would be best to leave tonight to get there in plenty of time for the wedding.' We couldn't believe our ears! A six-hour drive from England to Scotland, after sitting on a plane for nearly two days. My uncle had borrowed a little car for us to use while we were there, so we put the gear in the back and off up the M6 we went. Bill turned to me and said, 'Just keep talking, yell, tap me on the head, pull my ears, just keep me awake.' It was a bloody long drive, but I howled my eyes out in total joy when we crossed the border into bonnie Scotland after thirteen years.

We arrived at my granny's house quite late that night and it was so strange to open her front door and walk inside—with my husband this time. We were exhausted after travelling for three days so we dumped our gear on the floor and went straight to bed. I awoke to loud knocking at my granny's front door at her 'wee hoose' in Kirkcaldy the next morning. Granny Jackson had been placed in a nursing home by this stage and we were going to pick her up to take her to the wedding with us. I opened the front door and three of my Scottish aunties were vying for position on the doorstep in a haze of taffeta, veiled hats, and perfume. 'Och lassie, how ye have grown, so braw tae see een.' I was hugged and kissed and squeezed within an inch of my life. I greeted them all and introduced Bill. They were all laughing at our Australian accents and said that they felt like they were in an episode of *Neighbours*, which was huge in the UK at the time. My cousins even came home from work to watch it at lunchtime.

Bill and I went to see my granny with most of my aunties and cousins in tow. I saw her straight away, waiting for us to arrive, with her powderpuff white hair and pale blue suit, complete with a white rose on her lapel, all jazzed up for the wedding. I ran up and gave her the biggest hug with tears streaming down my face. 'I told you I would come back,' I sniffled into her shoulder. We stayed in that embrace for what seemed like hours. I was so happy to see my granny again.

Sitting in the church with all the Scottish side of the family felt like a dream. I had to pinch myself to make sure it was happening. My cousin was a stunning bride and her new husband wore a kilt and full Scottish traditional dress. We laughed and toasted the bride and groom. I got up and sang 'When I Fall in Love' by Nat King Cole with four of my aunties in three-part harmony without any rehearsal. What a brilliant day it was! I sat and wrote to Dad when I got back to Granny's place, telling him all the latest family news. It was so fantastic to be back 'hame' in Scotland again. I remembered the note that I had written in 1975 and pushed under a loose board behind the loo in Granny's bathroom. I went to look for it, and it was still there thirteen years later. It said, *If you are reading this in the future I am glad that you made it back,* and *Are the Bay City Rollers still popular?* Bill and I had a great laugh about this.

We travelled to Aberdeen and caught the North Sea ferry to Shetland. Once again, I was seasick all the way to Lerwick, the capital of Shetland. I spent the voyage lying on my bunk in our cabin feeling green while Bill downed whisky in the ferry bar. My gorgeous cousin, Brenda, and her new husband, Gordon, were rapt to meet us at the ferry terminal and we hugged each other in total glee. While I was staying with Brenda and Gordon, I cooked our evening meals to 'do my bit' as a helpful guest. Before I left Shetland, I wrote down all my recipes in a journal and gave them to Brenda as a thank-you gift. She had enjoyed my lasagne in particular and said that she would learn how to make it. Many pints and whisky chasers were consumed as we toured around visiting the rellies. Shetlanders are such welcoming, kind people and Bill thought he was in heaven! One night we were at the Lerwick Pub and an old guy came up and asked me if I was related to his old best mate. It turned out that Poppa and he had been friends for many years and played together in The Forty Fiddlers. A huge evening ensued with many people shaking my hand to say they were my cousin once removed or knew my mum's family. I think we visited every pub on the main island of Shetland and quite a few on the other three islands as well!

Brenda and Gordon took us to the ferry terminal three times because the weather was shocking, and the ferry couldn't sail because of the gale-force winds. We were secretly pleased each time the ferry got cancelled because we got to stay for another day. Every time I leave Shetland, I feel like my heart is going to break. The landscape is so majestic and stark as Shetland is quite treeless due to the fierce winds. It is both terrifying and hauntingly beautiful at the same time. There is such honesty and humbleness in the people; they are just the kindest people I have ever met. I just don't know how Nanna and Poppa found the courage to leave this incredible place. Once more, I told Brenda that I would return, and we set sail back to Aberdeen in Scotland.

We did a tour of whisky distilleries and I drove Bill from one dram of whisky to the next. I love the Scottish Highlands and we were quite bemused that we had covered all the places we wanted to see in about two days instead of the week we had allocated. After our Scottish tour of pubs, we returned to Kirkcaldy, to say goodbye to my granny. I knew that this would be the last time I would ever see my bonnie, wee granny. I think that sometimes you just know things without being told. I had seen my Scottish granny on three separate occasions in my life, once on her only trip to Australia in 1967 and twice in Scotland, and I could not have loved her more. She was so kind, warm-hearted, and generous. I had never seen her cross and would always remember her powdery smell and soothing hugs. I turned around at the door to her room to sear the image of her sitting by the window, hands folded in her lap into my brain. Once again, I was in tears all the way down the M6 to Oxford in England.

Four days of touring the pubs of London and staying in Earls Court, where Aussie tourists were plentiful, was great training for a twenty-eight-day Contiki tour of Europe. Our hotel room in London was tiny and had a shower in the corner next to the bed. There was no shower curtain or partition of any sort, so when we had a shower the carpet got soaked.

We commenced the Contiki tour in London. Our first stop was Paris, and my eyes were 'out on stalks' looking at the grandeur and architecture of this magnificent, historical city. It was everything and more that I had ever imagined the 'city of love' to be. I was swept away by the street artists and their amazing chalk drawings of famous paintings, the stylish Parisian ladies with their red lips and stiletto heels, the markets, the food; just the excitement of being a twenty-five-year-old Aussie in Paris for the first time. We stayed in a caravan park on the outskirts of the city which didn't enhance the ideal Parisian experience, but we made the most of it. Bill got blind drunk on a bottle of duty-free grog and passed out on our first night there. I swore if I ever came back to Paris again in the future, I would stay somewhere really flash on the Champs Elysées. Fast forward to my well-deserved 'retirement trip' in 2020 with a week's accommodation in a flash apartment near the Eiffel Tower all paid for in advance. *Stuff you, COVID-19!*

'Aussie, Aussie, Aussie, oi, oi, oi,' was the common bus mantra pulling into our many European destinations. We would drink as much as possible in every location before getting on the bus the next morning hungover and sleeping until we arrived at our next port of call. I had taken my pillow with me on the trip and I was offered twenty pounds or more every day by one of our fellow travellers to 'borrow' it. There were several other married couples on the bus and we all got on well and partied hard. Our fifth wedding anniversary was in spectacular Lauterbrunnen, Switzerland. The scenery was so majestic with cascading waterfalls and sheer mountain peaks that stretched up into the clouds. The crew held a mock wedding for us, complete with a white sheet for my wedding dress. Roy Rodgers, our bus driver, was the minister and we partied on into the wee small hours. Too hungover to go on the Eiger Mountain tour the next day, we stayed in bed nursing our hangovers.

'*Eins* to the *Mitte, Eins* to the *Titte, Eins* to the suck, suck, suck, *Prost!*' The bar of the accommodation we were staying at in Austria was noisy, loud, and cramped. Bill had just spent eighty pounds playing drinking games and shouting his mates schnapps chasers and I was furious! We didn't speak for a couple of days after this and there is a pic of me on a chair lift coming down a mountain, arms folded, glaring at Bill as he was heading up the mountain taking my photo. I reckon that half of the money we spent on this trip was on grog. The following week, in Rome, I was keen to go and have a look at Vatican City and the Sistine Chapel. I looked around the place we were staying and found Bill firmly ensconced in a deck chair by the pool, beer in hand. I asked, 'Are you coming with me on the Vatican tour?'

Bill replied, 'Naaa, I think I will just stay here and check out the tits.' Topless girls were sunbaking nearby. He certainly wasn't setting his sights on 'husband of the year'.

We left the Contiki tour in Amsterdam after a memorable night in the red light district where Bill was chosen to 'assist' the performer on stage by lying down shirtless while she drew a love heart on his chest with a texta inserted into her vagina. I was quite concerned about what she was going to do next, but she moved on to her next victim. Phew! We slept for nearly eighteen hours straight when we found our *pensione*. After partying hard for twenty-eight days, we were bloody exhausted. Bill was in his element in the Hog's Breath Cafe, as smoking joints was legal in Amsterdam.

Two Eurorail passes later, we pulled up at Munich Station and found a nice *pensione*. We befriended a couple of Canadian girls who were also staying, and they invited us to go with them to the opening of a new bar just around the corner. The White Lion Bar served 'White Lions,' which were rum, grenadine, and ouzo from memory. They were very strong, anyway, and after a couple of them, I felt a bit woozy, so I decided to go back to the *pensione* by myself.

Bill stayed on with our new friends drinking and when I woke up at three am and he hadn't returned I was worried. I ran into the Canadian girls' room and said, 'Hey, wake up, did Bill leave the bar with you guys?'

They said that he was still drinking when they left a couple of hours ago. I was frantic and scared about what to do. I had visions of him being mugged or worse and having to make the phone call to my parents-in-law in Australia to tell them. Just as I was about to call the Australian consulate, I heard a faint 'Help me' outside the window. I looked outside and down two floors, and there was Bill, spewing in the gutter. I rushed outside to help him, feeling simultaneously extremely pissed off and very relieved.

Salzburg was our next stop, and we found an Aussie-run backpackers and settled in. On the first night, they were holding an 'Aussie night' in the bar, and we met three nineteen-year-old girls from Queensland—called Jen, Fi, and Nat—who were also backpacking around Europe. We hit it off straight away and the next morning they came up to our room and asked us where we were going next. We were heading to Yugoslavia, as we wanted to go to Dubrovnik. They asked, 'Can we come with you?' So, off we went to the bus station and set off to Yugoslavia. The girls jokingly referred to us as 'Ma and Pa', as we were five years older than them. Dubrovnik was sensational and we stayed with a lady we called 'Mrs. Dubrovnik' (because we couldn't pronounce her name) in her house in the old quarter.

The food in Dubrovnik was awful! It was still a communist country then and you had to queue up at the bakery to get stale bread. I had always hated olives, but we learned to eat Mrs. Dubrovnik's olives and drink her homemade sangria instead of starving. We had to pass a knackery on our way back to Mrs. Dubrovnik's house and the smell was disgusting. We used to cover our faces with our towels or sarongs and run past it as fast as we could. I will never forget that smell.

After three weeks of getting on and off trains, lugging our backpacks up and down hills to find accommodation, drinking, sunbathing, and generally having the time of our lives, we had to say goodbye, as Bill and I were heading to the Greek islands. We promised to stay in touch and swapped addresses.

Chapter 8
The patter of little feet

B ill and I continued playing in a band. We had a new lineup by
this time and played a lot of British-influenced music, like The
Pretenders, The Stones, and The Who. The band was called 'Oxford
Circus' and we continued playing most weekends around the pubs in
Warrnambool. This afforded us a lot of extra cash, and we decided to
go to Hawaii for a holiday in July 1990.

We stayed in Waikiki for a week and then caught a boat to Kauai
for the second week. I loved the island and there was a little village
there called Hanalei which was the name of the place where Puff the
Magic Dragon supposedly lived. I had played the song, written by
Peter, Paul, and Mary, nearly every day of my teaching career, so I
thought it was very special to visit the actual location. The tiny pub
there also served delicious seafood chowder, so we ate there several
times that week.

Back at home, sitting in my favourite spot by the picture window
in my kitchen, smoking a fag and reading *Women's Weekly* in August
1990, I was startled by the wall phone ringing above my head. It
was my doc on the phone saying, 'You know that pregnancy test we
did this morning? Well, it has come back positive.' I stubbed out
my cigarette straight away and sat in shock. I had forgotten to take
my birth control pills with me on the trip to Hawaii. I had started
feeling a bit off-colour but hadn't even considered being pregnant
after being on the pill constantly for almost twelve years. I was happy

about it, as I felt ready to start a family. We had been married for eight years by then and I was starting to worry that we wouldn't be able to have children. I wasn't sure if Bill would be pleased, because he liked our free and easy lifestyle. I knew a baby would change this. I was a bit worried about telling Bill that I was pregnant and paced the floor waiting until he got home from work. I saw him coming in the front door later that day and stood up to greet him.

He said, 'How did you get on at the doc this morning? Is it a tropical disease or some bug that you picked up in Kauai?'

I tentatively said, 'No, not quite. I have something that is quite life-changing, actually.' Bill looked worried until I started laughing and blurted out, 'We are going to have a baby, you dickhead.'

He grinned and said, 'Shit hot,' and we hugged.

I went cold turkey, not smoking or drinking. I had always said, 'There is nothing worse than seeing a pregnant woman smoking,' so I practised what I had preached. I also felt very ordinary for the first trimester and it took all my energy to go to school and teach. I was very excited about becoming a mum and spent a lot of time doing up the spare bedroom as a nursery and sewing a layette for the new baby. I drank sparkling apple juice in my wine glass which made me feel like I was still having a vino at the end of the day. Bill continued to smoke and drink in my presence until one night a mate of his was visiting and said, 'Your missus is having a baby, the least you could do is smoke outside.' I think that Bill was a bit startled by a mate of his saying this, but he did go outside to smoke after that.

I continued singing in our band, but I was exhausted and feeling sick in early pregnancy and I couldn't continue to teach full-time and perform on the weekends. I recall one gig early on in my pregnancy where I had to keep running off stage to throw up and I decided to pull the pin. We had a band meeting, and the guys were fine about putting Oxford Circus on hold until the baby was born and I was ready to perform again.

On AFL Grand Final day in September 1990, I was anxiously waiting outside my parents-in-law's house after walking around to see them. I was really upset that Bill had decided not to come with me to pre-natal classes and wanted them to have a chat with him about it. Collingwood had just won the premiership after a thirty-two-year drought. Bill had gone to watch the game at a mate's place and I was on my own as usual. I sat on the bench on their back porch for ages waiting for them to come home. Eventually, I walked home without talking to them because I didn't want them to think I was a whinger or a sook. I have always had this don't-bother-people attitude, and I think it stems from thinking that my worries or anxieties are not as important as other people's.

The previous week, pre-natal classes had commenced at the Warrnambool Base Hospital. On the evening of the first class, I said to Bill, 'Righto, are you ready to go to our first pre-natal class?'

Bill responded with, 'I was going out with the boys tonight, so I will give it a miss, I think.' I wasn't happy about this at *all*, as you can imagine, and I gave him a serve, saying, 'I am carrying our child and you have to support me by coming to pre-natal classes. This is more important than hanging around with your mates.' He didn't change his mind and went out with his friends somewhere. I was bloody cross and I went to the class by myself. He didn't accompany me to any of the classes and I befriended a lovely lass there who was in the same boat, and we became each other's birth coaches. I was worried about Bill's lack of care and concern for me and our baby. I thought that he just needed time to get used to the idea and I tried hard not to be upset with him. I realise now that this was unacceptable behaviour, and I should've stood my ground more at Bill's lack of respect and care for both me and our baby.

Half asleep, going to the loo in early April 1991 I realised that my waters had broken. I woke Bill and he took me to the hospital. He left me there and went home again to bed. I was scared because

I had never been to a hospital before. I lay awake for hours feeling very anxious and frightened on my own. My contractions were non-existent by the next morning, so they put me on a drip to speed things up. Not much happened for quite a while. Bill had thoughtfully decided to come back, which I was pleased about. I could say something quite indignant, but I will just let my story unfold.

A very long night ensued. I was in and out of the shower as the water eased the terrible pain in my back. I almost sucked the nitrous oxide tank dry to lessen the pain. The baby, who had been in the correct position for delivery only the day before, had turned sideways or to a transverse position, and I couldn't push him out. After many failed attempts at pushing, an obstetrician was called in at three in the morning to deliver the baby. I remember the frantic faces above me and my GP looking way out of his depth and scared. The pain was overwhelming by this stage; I had no pain relief and I had an 'out of body' experience. I was standing on top of a cliff at Thunder Point, watching the waves crash against the rocks below. I remember my hair being whipped around my face. I then recall the obstetrician cutting me with scissors and putting something that looked like a tyre changer inside me and turning the baby around. Then forceps were used to deliver our precious baby boy.

Baby Jim lay on the delivery table looking over at us, really looking *hard* at us. It was almost as if he was thinking, *Ahh, so that's what they look like.* Then he went to sleep for three days. He had a pointy head and two black eyes from his very traumatic delivery. The poor little guy must've had a shocking headache and they whisked him away to check him out and make sure he was okay. I lay on the delivery table for a while then got up and walked back to my hospital room, trailing blood along the floor.

I couldn't sleep in the hospital. I was in a four-bedroomed ward, and it was very noisy. I was very sore, very tired, and overwhelmed by the number of visitors, cards, and flowers being delivered. This went on for seven days, and I was a basket case.

Sobbing my eyes out, one week after Jim was born, I was waiting for Bill to come and pick us up from the hospital. The boys had been out the previous night to 'wet the baby's head' and no-one could find Bill anywhere. Finally, Bob tracked him down, sleeping it off at home, and he came to the hospital to pick us up. I was very fragile by this stage. The hospital staff were quite concerned about me and told Bill so. Once home and taking the baby capsule out of the car, I realised that it had just been sitting on the back seat and had not been properly fitted. I sat in my feeding chair in the nursery with the baby and had a full-blown panic attack. I only know this now because I had never experienced anything like this before. I was shaking from head to toe and yelled for Bill to come and take the baby. I had never felt so anxious in my life and I was scared.

Baby Jim cried, no, screamed a lot. I had trouble breastfeeding him, probably because I was so wound up and anxious all the time. I felt very strange like I was walking around in a fog-like pea soup and because of my 'perfectionism', I tried hard to pretend that I was a capable, totally confident, young mum. I was terrified of hurting the baby, unsure why he cried and screamed so much, and berated myself for being a hopeless mother.

Out walking with Jim in the pram, we crossed the train bridge near our house, and I had this awful feeling that I was going to throw the baby off the bridge. I was shaking and crying and so frightened for myself. I made an appointment to see my doc straight away when I got home, emphatically telling him that I *had* to be seen that day. I told him that I was feeling very unwell, and that I thought I might have postnatal depression. He listened with a superior look on his face and said, 'Oh, it is very normal to feel a bit out of sorts after you have had a baby. Just give things some time to adjust and settle down.' I *hope* that new mums are listened to and supported far more these days and that doctors are trained more thoroughly to recognise the signs of postnatal depression. I battled along for many months in a black hole feeling very ill and mentally unstable.

The following year I returned to school, teaching part-time at Warrnambool Primary School. I felt that I needed to return to teaching to give me some grounding and a sense of who I was before I had Jim. I had lost my identity and sense of self. Mum was happy to care for Jim while I went back teaching part-time, and I was extremely grateful once again for my wonderful, supportive family. She knew that I had been struggling and like always, was trying to help me in any way she could.

It was so different from the smaller schools I had taught in and there was a committee for every single thing. Many of the teachers had been there for most of their careers and I was told quite often, 'This is how we do things, and this is the way things have always been done.' I tried my best to fit in, but I had never been a fan of strictly following the rules, so I was always defending myself and trying to suggest new ways of doing things. Life at home had become more stable and baby Jim thrived and was a happy little guy.

Early in 1993, I started to feel unwell one day and I knew that I was pregnant again before I even took a test. I was apprehensive about having another baby and becoming a basket case again, but the pregnancy was very easy, and I was as fit as a fiddle.

Nineteen ninety-three was the year that the Victorian Government, under Jeff Kennett's leadership, was slashing the funding for schools, and I was worried that if I took an extended period of leave I would lose my position. I taught right up until six weeks before the baby was born. I was convinced that it was another boy because there had been no girls born on Bob's side of the family for a long time. Bob was a twin himself and one of five brothers.

Bill, Jim, and I went to Lorne for a break when I commenced family leave. It coincided with our tenth wedding anniversary. We drove down to Apollo Bay on August 20 and had lunch in a pub where a mate of Bill's was head chef. I was feeling very large and uncomfortable by this stage and not keen on any physical intimacy. 'Where is my anniversary present?' I asked Bill, expecting a nice card or something to mark the occasion. I had been declining his advances because I was just so big.

'You don't deserve a present,' was his reply.

I sat and cried in the car all the way home. Once more, the voice in my head was loud and clear: *You aren't worthy.*

*

I was two weeks overdue, the size of a house, and I hadn't felt the baby move for a couple of days. I went to the hospital, and they put me on the foetal heart monitor. They told me to go home and get my things and come back. It was the AFL Grand Final day again and Bill had gone to watch it at a mate's place ... again! I watched the grand final that day sitting in my hospital room alone. Nothing was happening, and I was induced the following morning. Bill had decided to show up and be present for the baby's birth. The birth was very quick and when I asked the doctor how 'Matthew' was doing, he said, 'The baby is fine, but that is a strange name for a girl.' We had only thought of names for a boy because we were so sure that this baby would also be male. We had a couple of girls' names picked out 'just in case' thank goodness, but I hadn't bought any girly things or decorated the nursery in preparation for a girl.

Baby Ruby was like a perfect, porcelain doll. She had tiny ears that looked like pink seashells, a perfect bow-shaped mouth, and her skin was as soft as silk. I felt like I had won the lottery now that I had my 'pigeon pair'. She was an easy baby, would daintily have her milk, pull off with pursed lips, then go to sleep for hours and wake up cooing and smiling.

Bill was pleased that we had a daughter. I do think that he found it difficult having a girl though because he had never had a sister. His only experience of living with a female was with Berryl and me. I tried to encourage him to get really involved with taking care of his daughter, but he was reluctant and preferred looking after Jim, who was now two and a half. Jim had two speeds: flat out or asleep. He was an active little guy, and Bill would take him out to give me a break because I was very tired most of the time.

I was so relieved when the dreaded postnatal depression didn't return. I went back to school when Ruby was only six weeks old. It was quite difficult as I was breastfeeding and had to express my milk so my mum could feed her. Sometimes I had to go home at morning recess and lunchtime to feed Ruby. An old battleaxe who was acting principal summoned me up to her office to tell me that it was 'highly unprofessional to be leaving school to go home during the school day.' This was the attitude of my new place of employment: having a baby and breastfeeding was unprofessional.

Bill was becoming disillusioned with the nursing profession. Jeff Kennett had slashed hospital funding, too, and Bill wasn't happy about it. He was very interested in alternative medicine and decided to study naturopathy and return to full-time study in 1994. I thought that this was a bit strange because he smoked like a chimney and drank beer like a thirsty camel. He took a redundancy package from his nursing position and then I became the main breadwinner. I was extremely apprehensive about this and told Bill so. I didn't think it was a good idea because my anxiety was still very high. I was scared about having to support our family financially when I was so fragile. I attempted to explain this to Bill but once again he didn't listen or care. I soldiered on with a toddler and a baby, trying my best to keep my head above water, but I felt like I was drowning. I would often go to school with hardly any sleep because Bill didn't like getting up to the kids at night. I would teach all day and come home to a cranky husband and kids. *What in the hell did I teach today*, I would often think. I was so tired and stressed all the time.

I just kept on filling up my wine glass and going through the motions. I often think that if it hadn't been for my mum and her amazing support, I would've ended up in a psychiatric hospital. Ruby picked up on the tense vibes at home and she became quite a difficult child to manage, throwing tantrums and being very wilful. She would puff herself up and say to Bill, 'I don't like you, Daddy; you make my mummy cry in the toilet.' My little champion was trying to stick up for me. Bill was quite scared of Ruby at times when she stood her ground and said her piece.

Chapter 9
D.I.V.O.R.C.E

Nineteen ninety-five was a shocker of a year! My cousin committed suicide in March. Poppa passed away in May, and Nanna had a stroke in September. We were on holiday at Fi's grandmother's holiday house in Dickie Beach, on the Sunshine Coast in Queensland, when I was given the news (from a friend of Jen and Ian's as there was no phone in the old Queenslander house) that my nanna had died. I recall standing in the holiday house and watching a bird flying past the window, and I just knew I had to go back for her funeral; I wouldn't have been able to live with myself if I had not.

Bill wasn't exactly thrilled (I am being kind) that I was going to go home halfway through our holiday, but I stuck to my guns and booked a flight. It was almost impossible because it was the Thursday before the AFL grand final. I managed to book a seat and I recall that it cost $750, but I didn't care. Bill was cross with me for ruining our holiday, but for once, I stood up to him and said, 'Nanna was one of the most important people in my life and I am going home to pay my respects and support Mum.' I intended to return to Queensland to resume the holiday the day after the funeral.

Arriving home in Warrnambool, I realised that it was the first time that I had been in the house by myself since the kids were born. It was very quiet, so I did the ironing. I felt so torn leaving the kids and coming home and hoped that Bill would cope with looking after them by himself. Ruby had screamed the place down when she saw me packing my case and I was very fragile already. I didn't have to worry because Jen and Ian, Fi and Phil, came up from Brisbane and stayed at the holiday house to help Bill. I had never felt so grateful in my life. Ruby had just had her second birthday and she was hard work sometimes.

As I was sitting in the bar at Brisbane Airport having a vino or two before the flight, I had very mixed feelings about the state of our marriage, as I was physically and mentally worn out. I attended Nanna's funeral and the wake afterward at Nanna and Poppa's house. I felt that it was the end of an era now that my beloved grandparents had both passed away within three months of each other after sixty-four years of marriage.

There was some joy during this hard year when Sandy married her long-time boyfriend in November 1995 and I sang at her wedding ceremony. She was a stunning bride and Sally and I had a terrific time catching up with our old pals from our uni days and swapping stories about our exploits. Sally had a prosthetic leg by this stage and had travelled around the world, marrying a guy from Russia before returning to Australia to have her son. The marriage didn't last and she was living with her little boy in Koroit.

I was feeling like a 'frumpy mummy' in early 1996 and I decided to lose some weight. I had put on a fair bit of weight during my two pregnancies and weighed about seventy-five kilos. I am a 'short arse', standing at five foot two, so I was rapt after losing about twenty-five kilos with a popular weight loss company and I could now fit into my pre-mummy clothes. I felt good, and I hoped my new improved body would put some much-needed zing back into our fading marriage. We had been having marriage counselling to try to salvage our relationship, but it wasn't going well.

At one session the counsellor said, 'What nice things do you do for your wife, Bill, to acknowledge how hard she works in looking after you and your kids?' He looked a bit dumbfounded and mumbled something unintelligible.

I blurted out, 'All it would take is for you to make me a cup of tea and tell me to sit down and have a rest.' I ran from the room crying. My dad had made Mum a cup of tea every morning of their marriage and taken it to her before she got up. I saw this as saying, 'I care for you, and you are nurtured.' I wasn't nurtured, I wasn't appreciated, I was just part of the furniture.

We booked a trip to Bali without the kids to work on saving our relationship in September 1996. Ruby had just turned three, and Jim was five. Mum and Dad were happy to mind the kids while we went away for ten days. We arrived at Mum and Dad's place to drop the kids off, and Dad was complaining of a bad headache. Jane was there at the time and said, 'You just go and I will take Dad up to outpatients and get him checked out.' We drove to Melbourne and boarded our flight to Denpasar, Bali, via Sydney. When we arrived in Sydney, there was a message for me to go to the Qantas desk. I went to the desk and I was given the message that Dad had suffered a brain aneurysm and been airlifted to the Alfred Hospital in Melbourne. He was in a critical condition in intensive care. I was a blubbering mess, but the Qantas staff were wonderful, and they put us on the next available flight back to Melbourne. Once we arrived back at Tullamarine, I caught the Skybus back into the city and Bill drove home to Warrnambool to pick up the kids. Unbelievably, it was exactly a year after our Queensland holiday disaster, and we felt like we couldn't catch a break. Dad was in intensive care for a couple of weeks, but he made a great recovery and was allowed to go home. We had managed to change the booking details and we went to Bali a couple of months later.

Everything just felt 'off'. I was tired and couldn't seem to communicate to Bill how I felt. A diary entry from that time says: *My marriage is like a barren wasteland. I wonder if most people who have been married for nearly thirteen years forget the little things that make all the difference, a smile, a kind word, or a hug?*

Our holiday in Bali bought us some time and we soldiered on for the kids' sake, but I was just going through the motions by then. Home life was very volatile. I was trying hard to be a thoughtful and considerate wife, but I didn't feel like Bill was reciprocating. There was no affection or kindness, I was constantly exhausted with the demands of teaching, caring for Ruby and Jim, and doing most of the domestic tasks. We were arguing about stupid things and then not talking to each other for days at a time. I felt like I was a single parent already as Bill withdrew further and further from us. There is a photo of the kids dressed up as Santa in the lounge room looking excited for Christmas and Bill sitting on the coffee table staring ahead blankly, looking like he wished he was anywhere else.

Bill and I had been playing in a trio by this stage with a friend of ours who was an excellent pianist. We rehearsed in the room under our house, which was convenient because the kids would be in bed. I still loved performing and singing, but the strain of teaching, looking after two small children, and running a household became too much. We played at a popular venue in town until two o'clock in the morning one weeknight in 1997. I had to go to school the next day and take the kids to Mum's first. I got home from the gig and threw up from the anxiety and stress of trying to do it all. I sat down with Bill the following night and said, 'I can't play gigs anymore. I physically can't manage it with two small children, you, the house, and teaching.' I wasn't angry, I just told the truth and he seemed to accept it. He listened to what I said for once as I was quite calm while I spoke to him. My usual form had been to bottle things up, not wanting to upset the apple cart, and then explode when I could no longer contain my anger. He said that he had been thinking about starting a new band with some of his mates and would I be okay if he went ahead with that. I said, 'Fine, you keep playing because I know how much you enjoy it.' The trio wound up and Bill went back into rehearsal with a whole new band.

It was Warrnambool's 150th anniversary in 1997 and I had been asked to develop a performance to celebrate this. It was another huge task. I wrote a musical called *School Days*, which celebrated 150 years of our town's history. As Warrnambool Primary School is the oldest school in town, I developed the story around the past, present, and future of our school. It provided a distraction from my crumbling marriage and gave me some much sought-after validation that I could still be creative and produce something special. The show was a huge success, with packed performances at the Warrnambool Performing Arts Centre. Professionally, I was doing well. My private life was another matter, as we were arguing about anything and everything, not communicating at all and drinking too much, and I was miserable. I was sitting in the front porch at Mum and Dad's one Sunday after our roast lunch. I could hear everyone laughing and mucking around in the pool room. Dad popped his head around the door with a concerned look on his face and said in his broad Scottish accent, 'It is very difficult to watch one of your children being so unhappy.' Mum and Dad had never interfered in my marriage, but I knew that they were worried about me and how miserable I was. It was difficult keeping my anguish and sadness to myself. I just sat there and cried alone in the front porch in desperation.

During our marriage guidance counselling, the therapist had suggested that we needed to try to do more things together. It was always me taking the kids to the park or beach or their friends' places. Bill just seemed to be somewhere else when we did go and do things. My family had always done a lot together and I just couldn't understand why he didn't like being with us. Berryl had said to me, 'It isn't good to live in your family's back pocket.' I had no idea what she meant, but I realised that she thought I spent far too much time with my family. The Christmas that Bill suggested we go and pick up the kids' Christmas toys and do our last-minute shopping together, I was thrilled. Mum said that she would mind the kids and off we went.

Everything was fine; we picked up the kids' layby gifts, selected the presents for Bill's family (I usually did that, too), and decided to treat ourselves to a counter lunch at the pub. I was so happy that we were doing this together for a change and thought once again that maybe we were finally on the road to a better marriage.

We went to the Warrnambool Hotel for our lunch, and it was packed with people who had just done their Christmas shopping. I was in a terrific mood and looking forward to spending a lovely Christmas with my family. Sitting at the table in the pub, Bill pulled out an envelope and gave it to me to read. I was excited because I thought that he was giving me an early Christmas present like a gift voucher or maybe tickets to a Melbourne show. 'Goody, goody, I hope this is what I think it is?' I was smiling and looking excitedly at Bill. I opened the envelope in great anticipation of a lovely surprise. It turned out to be a sexual fantasy that Bill had dreamed up and written about that he wanted to re-enact in real life. It was so unexpected to receive this at a pub lunch after picking up the kids' toys. I felt trapped, upset, and unappreciated, and sat there chewing while my food turned to dust in my mouth. My happy mood instantly deflated. I felt my eyes welling up with tears and put on my sunglasses so people wouldn't see me crying. I wanted to run away and never come back. I couldn't even speak, I was so upset. My happy Christmas frame of mind and joy at picking up the kids' toys together was ruined. I walked out and went back to the car. We didn't speak for a couple of days after this. I pulled out my 'Academy Award' à la Emma Thompson in her *Love Actually* performance and put on a brave Christmas face for the kids.

Max, Bill's older brother, was turning forty in February 1998 and Aggie, his wife, was giving him a big party at their very flash house. It was a very smart occasion as Aggie was quite the entertainer and liked things to be 'just perfect'. Bill and I put on our glad rags and headed down to their place for the party. We were able to walk because it wasn't very far from our place. It was a swanky occasion, and we were having a great time. Bill was over talking to his surfing buddies from years before and I could hear raucous laughter coming from their side of the room. They were taking turns sculling something from a bottle and getting fairly pissed. The next minute I realised that Bill was standing on top of Max and Aggie's very expensive marble-topped coffee table, pretending to surf. His arms were flailing about to the pulsating music while he was 'hanging five'. Almost in slow motion, the table tipped on its side and there was a horrible splitting sound as the table hit the polished floorboards and smashed in two. I had my hand over my mouth in disbelief and it seemed that the room had frozen in silence. Bill jumped up and ran out the front door, leaving me to apologise and try to pick up the shattered table. I was mortified, as everyone was looking at me open-mouthed as if I had broken the table. I went looking for Bill; he had run up the hill and gone home. I found him in his den under the house and told him that he would have to reimburse Max and Aggie for the table, and gave him our cheque book. He was drunk, and I told him to go to bed and sober up because he was going down to their place first thing in the morning to apologise!

A couple of months later, the Queensland crew arrived. Jen and Fi and their husbands, Fi's brother, and his girlfriend were coming to stay with us for Easter. I was apprehensive because I knew that Bill and I were on the rocks. It was going to be difficult for me to pretend that everything was fine when in reality things were very tense and strained between us. I was so excited and set about getting the place ready. We had been up to Queensland a couple of times by then and they had visited us when Jim was a baby. What brilliant guests they were, jumping up to do the dishes, bath the kids, or just sit and chat with me. I said to them, 'I think my lucky star must have been following me when I met you in Salzburg ten years ago.' I do believe that there are people who you are meant to meet in life and these gorgeous women were my people.

Bill's new band was performing by then, so he was often at band rehearsals or off with his mates somewhere. I was sitting in the dining room one morning, and Fi said, 'I know things aren't great between you and Bill, and I hope you know the difference between physical and emotional abuse.' There is no way to hide a broken relationship when people are staying in your house. I was quite taken aback, but I sat with them and told them about some of the things that had happened. I hadn't opened up to anyone before this and I was worn down and defeated. Fi mentioned that she didn't like the way Bill spoke to me and how he wasn't very involved with me or the kids. He had gone to rehearsal while our visitors were staying and left me to entertain them all. I took note of what she said because she is a fair and genuine person and wouldn't bring this up if she wasn't concerned about me. This had an impact on me because I could see that my unhappiness wasn't just in my imagination and that it was obvious to other people as well.

We also went on a weekend trip to Queensland to attend the fortieth birthday party for Fred, our dear friend from our early band days. We surprised him by just showing up unannounced. He was rapt to see us but became aware very quickly that all was not well between Bill and me. I was quiet and withdrawn on this trip and he asked me if I was alright. I didn't go into huge detail, because I didn't want to spoil his happy celebration, but I did tell him that Bill and I weren't in a good place. He gave me a huge bear hug as we were leaving to go home and said, 'Always here for you, Magenta.'

During the July school holidays, I made an appointment to see my wonderful female GP. I had moved on from the other one in 1991, after his awful handling of my postnatal depression. I sat down and she asked, 'How are you?'

I broke down sobbing, struggling to breathe. Everything came pouring out of me. 'Teaching 640 kids a week, organising and running a household, getting up early every day to manage working and the kids, doing the bulk of the caregiving and chores, trying to keep in shape and look good, walking on eggshells all the time, and just the relentless voice in my head saying, "you are not worthy".' She cancelled all the remaining appointments she had that afternoon and just let me cry and talk.

She told me that I had been under extreme pressure and stress for a long time and that she would prescribe some antidepressants to help me cope better. This did relieve my stress and anxiety but I was still drinking while I was taking them so they weren't working as effectively as they should have. This was the first time that my depression and anxiety had been acknowledged and treated. I had battled along for years on my own and I was worn out.

I attempted to talk to Bill about what had transpired with my GP and I asked him to read my diary as I hoped it would help him to understand how I was feeling and how we could make things better. His written response was:

> I feel very ashamed of some of my behaviour in the past. Neglecting or ignoring your emotional needs is a form of abuse and I apologise deeply. I am pleased that you have sought help for your depression and I will support you in every way I can. I fully realise how hard you work at school (sometimes too hard) and recognise that you need some time out. I think that you should take responsibility for this. I also recognise that we need some time together. I am looking forward to our relationship growing as we continue to communicate and break down our barriers. I love you.

I was delighted when I read this response in my diary and I felt positive about our future for the first time in years.

In October 1998, Bill's new band was playing at a motorbike rally near the Boggy Creek Pub and he asked me if I would come and do the backup vocals for the gig. I agreed and drove out there with the car full of gear and helped set up. I felt like I had gone back in time to our early band days. Bill always got very anxious about the sound and gear being set up properly, he would get cranky and short with everyone, and I decided to just leave him to it and check out the motorbikes. While I was looking at the bikes a couple of guys came over to chat to me and try to pick me up. I was flattered but told them that I was married to the guy over there mucking around with the sound equipment. They said, 'He hasn't even looked over here once to see if you are okay. I wouldn't be doing that here if I was him.' It was a fairly wild event and girls were riding around topless on the back of bikes and there was a tent where you could go for some 'privacy'. It occurred to me that even total strangers now were commenting on the state of my marriage.

I would drive to school after racing around getting the kids ready, making lunches and dealing with the morning chaos while Bill sat downstairs in his den smoking and drinking a coffee. One day, Mum was going to come up and help me and I just sat on the end of my bed in tears. I was sinking fast and I didn't know what to do. I would drive to school crying, make a coffee in my classroom, sit behind my desk and try to compose myself, blow my nose, wave my magic wand and stand up and walk over to the door. The students would be lined up outside the Arts Centre eagerly waiting for me. I would plaster a smile on my face, open the sliding door and say, 'G'day everyone, what a fantastic day to learn, let's all sing *Puff the Magic Dragon.*' I remember thinking, *Give me that Academy Award now, Nicole Kidman!*

I struggled along valiantly for a long time and I even managed to take one hundred students to Wakakkiri, the primary school version of the Rock Eisteddfod, to perform our seven-minute item called *I Am Australian.* We won our regional heat in Geelong and made it through to the grand final in Melbourne. We had one hundred students performing, so we had to take two buses to Melbourne and that was very expensive. There was doubt about whether we would be able to go to the grand final because of the huge cost. The kids banded together and they organised an 'I Am Australian Day' at school.

Everyone dressed up as their favourite Aussie character and paid two dollars. I went as Dame Edna, Jim was a swagman, and Ruby dressed up as Nutsy Koala from *Blinky Bill*. It was a fantastic day and the kids raised more than enough money to pay for our buses to Melbourne. That was as fantastic as seeing the kids perform. I remember being on yard duty that day and watching a little prep student give one of the Wakakirri kids his pocket money. The little guy didn't want to buy anything, he just wanted to make sure the 'big kids' got to go to the final. Watching the students performing on stage at the Melbourne Arts Centre was amazing. I stood in the wings watching my fabulous students with tears rolling down my face; they gave it everything they had that night. We didn't win the competition, but I have never been so proud of a group of students in my life. It was a very exciting time professionally, but my personal life was miserable.

Two weeks later, I decided I would like to go to the movies to see a show and have a break. Bill was at home with the kids and I felt pleased that he had acknowledged that I deserved some 'time out' now and then. When I arrived home around eight o'clock, he wasn't there. The kids were both in bed sleeping but Bill had gone out and left them at home alone. I was bloody livid. By the time he got home from his mate's place, I was about to pack the kids up and leave. I told him that I was so disappointed in his selfish behaviour and that I couldn't believe he would go out and leave the kids at home by themselves.

'You always put yourself first. You are a selfish husband and an awful father!' I screamed at him. 'I am fucking sick of it, I cannot and *will* not live a life of abuse anymore. You have two beautiful kids and a wife that loved you, hoping and praying that you would notice her—you just don't care—you have turned your back on us, your own *family!* No, it is worse than that—you have betrayed *us* and you have treated *me* with total fucking contempt. I want out.'

A couple more weeks of pretending went by until we could both no longer deny that our marriage was totally beyond repair.

Bill and I separated in November 1998. On the actual day we split up, there was no huge argument or any yelling at all. I had just got home from my Saturday morning step aerobics class and Bill was smoking in the room downstairs. I went in and said calmly, 'I have been really unhappy for a long time and I think it is time for us to separate.' He asked me if I wanted him to leave and I said, 'Yes.' I took the kids over to Jane's house to give him some time to pack some things. Mum and Dad were there, and I ran up to Dad and just started sobbing.

The kids and I went to stay with Mum and Dad in their holiday house in Port Fairy for a couple of weeks so I could let the dust settle and just have a rest. Bill realised that this time there was no reprieve. He sent flowers and came over to see me, but I had made my decision. I couldn't face any more emotional abuse, flagrant contempt of my trust, and total disrespect. I remained in our house with full custody of the kids and Bill went to Melbourne to re-establish himself there.

It was strange being a single mum and looking after the kids by myself. Jim did miss his dad and I tried to reassure him that his daddy leaving had nothing to do with anything he had done. He was such a sweet and loving little boy. I gave him lots of cuddles and made sure he was well-loved by his mummy. Ruby didn't seem upset and continued being bossy and wilful. She was at kindergarten by this time and loved a Brigadoon puppet doll there called 'Keisha'. She would have to get there early on the days she went to kinder to make sure that no-one else played with 'my dolly'. I had a chat on the phone with Santa that year and guess who was sitting on the lounge room step dressed in her coat and hat with adoption papers in her hand on Christmas morning? I will never forget the look of pure joy on Ruby's face when she ran down the passage in her jammies and saw her favourite doll sitting on the lounge room step.

Chapter 10
New beginnings

Over the summer holidays of 1998/99 I reconnected with Tom, the teacher that I had met at Somers school camp in 1987. He had just separated from his wife and they had shared custody of their two teenage daughters. We had hit it off straight away all those years ago. He invited me out for dinner and I accepted. Our relationship blossomed very quickly and I was quite swept off my feet by being treated nicely and given respect and courtesy. We became an item and spent all our spare time together.

He stayed at my house when his girls were with their mother and I managed a couple of nights here and there when his girls stayed with him. I desperately wanted our relationship to work and ignored a few 'red flags' at the beginning. I had taken up smoking again on the trip to Bali. I just lit a fag one day by the pool like it was the most normal thing in the world. Tom hated smoking and it was an ultimatum: the fags or him. At a flash masquerade ball party in Ballarat to welcome in the new millennium, I butted out my final cigarette at five minutes to midnight on 31 December 1999.

My family all thought that Tom was a great guy and they got on like a house on fire. I was pleased about this after years of doing everything with the kids by myself. He was seventeen years older than me, but at the time I didn't see that as a problem. His maturity and calm nature were very refreshing after living with 'Peter Pan' for so many years. He didn't like disorder at all, and look out if you messed up his car. Jim had just narrowly squeezed by it in our driveway on his bike one day and Tom nearly had a heart attack, thinking that Jim had scratched his car.

He was also a 'man's man' and belonged to the Beer and Beef Club, a men-only club that met once every couple of months to drink beer and eat beef. I joked that I was going to start up a 'Chardonnay and Cheese Club' for the ladies, but it never eventuated. He enjoyed music and he knew that I had been a singer in several bands. He wasn't keen for me to perform again when an old band member asked if I would sing at a fundraiser for a charity he was sponsoring. He thought that it wasn't very dignified to sing in pubs. I thought that was odd, but I toed the line.

After fifteen months of running all over town with my two primary-aged children, going back and forth between two households, and juggling Tom's teenagers and their hectic schedules, we decided to sell both our homes and buy one house together. I was quite sad about selling my beloved house that I had put so much time, care, and effort into. I had suggested to Tom that we could build on to my place to make room for his girls, but he wasn't keen on that idea. I even had plans already drawn up for an extension by an architect that Bill and I had been going to use. He wrinkled his nose and said, 'Too many old sheds and pokey rooms here.' Another red flag and a big insult to me after all the years of hard work it had taken to create a modern, functional home out of a dated old dump.

My house went on the market in January 2000. Oh, how I *hated* that big For Sale sign on my front lawn. Bill was wanting his share of our assets by then and was being extremely difficult to negotiate with. I agreed to a fifty/fifty split, even though I was awarded full custody of Jim and Ruby. Bill wanted half of my superannuation, but I stuck to my guns and said, 'No way,' as I realised that one day this might be my only asset. The house sold within a week to a lovely couple.

The day the kids and I left our home was one of the saddest days of my life. Jim and I got up early and watched the sunrise from our front deck together for the last time. I couldn't close the door behind me and I cried in the car to the new place Tom and I had bought together in the northern part of town. I hoped that I was making the right decision in selling my home and moving in with Tom. Our new house was large and spacious, roomy enough for six people, and very well appointed and finished. My kids had their own rooms and TV room.

Tom's girls had their own rooms and bathroom that we had especially built adjoining the huge garage. We had a parents' retreat, and the kids were not allowed in this space. Tom was very particular about tidiness and the place being immaculate. I thought my neat freak ways were over the top, but he took it to a whole new level.

He played golf every Saturday while I spent the day ferrying kids to their part-time jobs and sporting activities, doing housework, cooking dinner, making sure his beer was in the freezer chilling, and filling the spa bath before he arrived home. I would prepare our evening roast and enjoy several glasses of wine in the process. He began to quiz me about how much I was drinking, but I was very good at fobbing him off. I had a secret stash that I kept on standby, so I didn't have to open the bottle in the fridge chilling for our evening meal. I recall Ruby at eight years old asking me, 'Do most mummies drink lots of wine like you?'

My GP had suggested some counselling for me after my separation and impending divorce from Bill. This therapist was in Melbourne and I drove down to see her monthly for about twelve months. I had a lot to process after my marriage ended and drinking lots of wine was just a band-aid to mask my pain and sadness. Tom also noticed that I was very fond of vino but it hadn't caused any problems at that stage, and I was still fronting up for school bright-eyed and bushy-tailed, looking after my two babies and Tom's girls when they stayed with us and enjoying a new, exciting relationship.

I had given my psychologist my old diaries to read and she was quite amazed that I had stayed with Bill so long. I remember her saying to me, 'Bill never left the rock band and didn't grow up. He wouldn't accept his responsibilities as a husband and a father and expected you to carry the whole burden.' Yes, that was true, I had shouldered the lot for years and I had just accepted it as my lot in life.

Conversations about Bill's lack of emotional intelligence brought her to the conclusion that he was quite possibly struggling with how to express his feelings to me and the kids. I thought back to his past behaviours and felt that she was probably correct. I was being 'punished' for my defection from our marriage at this stage and I can recall one phone conversation where I was told, 'I wouldn't piss on you if you were on fire!'

It didn't take long for his true colours to appear. Jim and Ruby suffered the most throughout this period and I tried to keep life as stable as possible for them, keeping to our normal routines, going to school, and seeing my family. I offered to take the kids around to Bill's parents so they could spend time with them, but I never heard a word back. I was wiped off the face of the earth after twenty-one years of being a part of their family. I did not get one phone call from Max or Aggie to see if the kids and I were okay. This hurt me greatly after being a kind and helpful sister-in-law and aunty for many years. I did not get one opportunity to discuss my side of the story or explain what had happened. I know that if the situation had been reversed, I would've had the decency to reach out and show some kindness.

Our divorce became final in July 2000. Mum and Dad came with me to the court hearing to support me. When we left the courtroom, Dad said, 'I suppose I will have to take you back again,' winked at me, and hugged me. I had a flashback to us sitting in the bridal car seventeen years before and hugged him back. I said to Tom that I was glad that I had closed that chapter of my life and was moving forward into my new chapter. 'When will you go ahead with your divorce?' I asked him.

He replied, 'I don't care if we never divorce; I am never getting married again.'

It was like being punched in the stomach. I had assumed that we would both divorce and get married within a reasonable amount of time. Boy, I was pissed off. I went for a run along the beach, tears streaming down my face and berating my bloody stupidity once more. I was just a bloody maid who looked after his girls and house with added benefits.

I was very sad during this time and I decided to go to Sydney to see Fred and his wife as I needed to have a break away. Bill wanted to see the kids in the winter school holidays, so I took them down to Melbourne, dropped them at his place, and hopped on a plane to Sydney, where I enjoyed playing the tourist. It was an interesting time to be there because it was just before the Sydney Olympics and the city was being polished and shined. A radio ad was encouraging people to 'sweep your front yards and fix your fences'. The place was a hive of activity.

I set myself three tasks on this trip as a way of saying goodbye to my marriage and moving forward with my life. I challenged myself to do three things that I had never done before that made me scared. The first task was to do the Sydney Harbour Bridge Climb and sing the national anthem under the Australian and Olympic flags in the centre at the top of the bridge. I have never been a fan of heights, so this was a scary concept. There were lots of Asian tourists on my climb and when I started singing 'Advance Australia Fair,' they all started taking pictures, thinking that this was an actual part of the experience! One of the couples was celebrating their fortieth wedding anniversary and told me that I had made it very special for them.

My second task was to go to Kings Cross and buy something from a sex shop. I nervously entered a rather seedy-looking place and approached the counter. I saw a row of X-rated videos on a stand and decided that I would purchase one. I handed it over to the shop assistant and he said quite loudly, 'Ahh, *Debbie Does Dallas*, an oldie but still a goodie.' I shoved the video in my bag and quickly exited the shop with my face on fire.

Task three was to go out for dinner to a flash restaurant by myself. I took the ferry to Watson's Bay and went to Doyle's Seafood Restaurant. I sat at my table for one and ordered my delicious seafood and wine. I had my diary and I wrote about my experience while listening to the conversations of the diners around me. There was a rather posh lady sitting at the table next to me berating her daughter about something and the young lass was crying. I made sure that I glared at the old bat once or twice. It was different eating out in a flash restaurant by myself, but I felt empowered knowing that I didn't need a date or other people with me to treat myself. I travelled home feeling like I was ready to tackle the next phase of my life.

My friends invited me to go out with them one Friday night not long after my return from Sydney. We had always had a long-standing catch-up every Friday night. I hadn't seen them for quite a while because I was so busy, so they suggested that we have a drink together at the pub and then continue by going out for dinner. I assumed that the kids would be fine being at home with Tom while I had a night out, especially after all the running around I did with his daughters. I said to him, 'I hope it is okay if I go out with the girls on Friday night?'

He replied, 'Who is going to look after Jim and Ruby?' I thought he was kidding, and I said, 'You, of course; you will be home, won't you?' He was deadly serious when he said that it was his Friday night, too, and he deserved rest and wouldn't look after the kids. I was stunned and very cross about this and just walked out and slammed the door of the parents' retreat. I didn't go on my girls' night out, and this just added more fuel to my anger and disappointment.

Over the next eighteen months, I spent a lot of time in the study logging into chat rooms, a glass of vino by my side. I was hurt, once again feeling unworthy and cheap. I started buying casks of wine and hiding them in the drawer under my computer. One day, I started chatting to a guy from Sydney called Sam. He was a music teacher and had just separated from his wife. He was going through a tough patch, and we connected and had lots in common. He had two boys who his ex-wife wouldn't let him see and I felt sorry for him. We spoke online for a couple of months, and we decided to meet in real life as he was flying down to Melbourne. I had tried to talk to Tom about how I was feeling and why I was upset. He could be very one-eyed and just couldn't understand why I was feeling rejected and unappreciated. I was realising that I had made a big mistake diving head-first into a new relationship without having time on my own to work out who I was and what I wanted for myself.

Jim had footy training every Wednesday night. After being held up at a meeting at school, I rang Tom and asked him to pick him up. It was the middle of winter and very muddy on the footy oval. Tom had made Jim sit on old blankets on the back seat of his car and take off his muddy boots and clothes before entering the house. I can still see the poor little guy turning blue and shivering on the back porch. The guy was a physical education teacher for God's sake. I was incredulous.

I was nervous and excited driving down to Melbourne to meet Sam in May 2002. I was taking the kids to stay with Bill for a few days and meeting Sam for the first time. Driving up the ramp at Tullamarine to pick him up from the airport, my heart was in my throat. I recognised him straight away from his online photo, and we talked non-stop back into Melbourne. He was a lot of fun, and we walked around the city, stopped for a drink in quite a few bars, and enjoyed each other's company. It was just nice to have fun and laugh with no huge list of jobs to do or others to organise. I felt so joyful and young again. It was like taking a couple of days of 'time out' from my life. We walked around the city enjoying the sights, eating at nice restaurants, and feeling carefree. We said our goodbyes before I left to pick up the kids to go home, thinking that we wouldn't see one another again. But we continued to chat online, things at home didn't improve, and we decided to see one another once more.

Tom and I had planned a trip to Fiji with all the kids in the winter school holidays. I had also taken some long service leave to have a break from school. The week before the trip I met up with Sam again in Melbourne and we drove to a little coastal place nearby for a couple of days' break together. I had told my family and friends that I was spending a couple of days with some girlfriends that I hadn't seen for a long time. I know that this was very dishonest and I am not proud of it. I was just feeling so upset and angry at being treated like the hired help and I had started referring to myself as the 'maid.' It was revenge that fuelled my decision to meet Sam again, but it bit me on the bum. Tom ended up ringing one of my girlfriends' husbands and he found out that she was at home. The shit hit the fan and he wanted to know the truth and I told him. We ended up still going on the trip to Fiji, but it was our swansong. It just wasn't right between us, and when the kids and I arrived home separately, we went to stay with my mum and dad for a couple of weeks.

I felt like I had gone full circle and ended up where I had started in my old bedroom at home. It was a strange time and I wasn't sure what to do next. In the local paper one day, a two-bedroomed unit was advertised for private rent. I rang up the guy straight away and we went to have a look. The rent was very reasonable, so I signed the lease and moved in.

My drinking had escalated at this stage. I was a single mum trying to support two kids and keep our heads above water. Tom had remained in the house we bought together, and it was a real legal battle to get him to pay me out. It took fifteen months of seeing a solicitor get him to agree on a settlement figure. House prices had just gone through the roof in the early 2000s. I was only given the money I had contributed to buying the property, even though it was now worth much more than what we originally paid for it. Screwed over once more, I just tried my best to keep going for the kids.

I drove up to Sydney with the kids several times to stay with Sam. He lived with his elderly father and younger brother in a house his father had built in the fifties. It was strange walking up the hill to the shops and being able to see the Sydney Harbour Bridge in the distance. His mum had passed away several years ago from cancer and I always got the feeling that they had never got over it. Sam's brother was approaching forty and acted like a teenager. He was going out with a sixteen-year-old girl, and I thought that this was very inappropriate.

I knew that Sam liked to smoke dope and I watched him have bongs several times in his brother's apartment downstairs. I didn't partake as I had given up smoking dope after my uni days. Dope had never agreed with me anyway and I preferred to drink my wine. Sam was partial to a drink as well, so we drank quite a bit during our times together.

I attended Allan's wedding to his long-time partner in September of that year and was quite mortified to see Tom there as well. I drank far too much bubbly, and this was not good because I was also videotaping the service and reception that day. Watching the video back is cringeworthy as I am laughing like a hyena and the camera work gets increasingly jumpy as the video goes on. Jane was really cross with me about being drunk at the wedding. She called me the following week and we had 'words' about this on the phone. Once again, my family and I had a very strained relationship for a while.

Chapter 11
Single motherhood

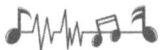

Being a single mum is really hard work. I had never imagined that I would ever be a single parent. I know that I tried my best, but I made a lot of mistakes. One thing I do know is that there was not one single day where I didn't love my kids with my whole heart. If someone had to go without something, it was me. If the chop was burnt, I ate it. I kept a roof over our heads, decent clothes on our backs, and good food in our bellies. School was very tough at this point because I had so much going on in my head. I would get home from school, go straight to the fridge, and pour a glass of wine. Ruby had to share my bed because it was a two-bedroom unit, but it was nice hearing her breathing beside me every night. Jim was entering his later primary school years and was quite cross with me at this stage, I think. I recall him saying to me, 'I don't like living in a unit.' It wasn't an easy time. I was quite lonely and very worried about what was going to happen to us.

Sam surprised me by coming down from Sydney for my fortieth birthday. I had no idea that he was going to come. I took him to meet Mum and Dad, but Dad wouldn't even come out of the kitchen to meet him. I realised that he was very upset with me for the breakdown of my relationship with Tom and for moving the kids around again.

My fortieth birthday dinner was held at a restaurant in town and it was an awkward evening. I drank heaps to dampen my anxiety and no-one in the family spoke to Sam at all. Sandy also happened to be there celebrating her birthday, so we took off to the pub together after our families had gone home. It was a big night, as I recall. We ran into Paul Jennings at the pub and had a chat about our uni days. Sandy and I told him that he was our favourite lecturer when we were at uni and I remember telling him that I was going to write a book one day and he laughed. I said a tad drunkenly, 'I *will* write a book, Paul, and then you can read my book.' Chatting to Paul recently, I was surprised to learn that he remembered this incident. Well, here is the book, Paul!

Sam got on well with my friends and we arrived back at my unit very inebriated early the next morning. The kids had been staying with Allan and his wife overnight. I knew that they were all pissed off with me and we kept a wide berth from each other during the rest of that year.

I am terrible at asking for help. I think it is a 'pride' thing. I was struggling by this stage and I didn't have anyone to confide in apart from Sam. We spent a lot of time messaging one another or speaking on the phone. My mobile bill was astronomical, so we began calling each other on the landline after nine when long-distance calls were cheaper. I felt like he was the only person who could understand what it was like, being a single dad himself. This bonded us and we continued flying up and down to visit one another for about fifteen months.

Sam and I decided to spend Christmas together in Sydney in 2003. Bill was going to come home from Melbourne, and he wanted to have Jim and Ruby for the day. I decided to go, but I was apprehensive about not being with my kids for Christmas for the first time; it just seemed weird. It was strange having Christmas lunch with a different family. I thought about my kids constantly, and I hoped that they were okay.

Ruby still remembers this Christmas as her worst ever! She said that Santa didn't come to Nanny's house, and it nearly broke my heart. Every year since they had been small, I had stayed up until the wee hours of Christmas Day to make the lounge room look like Santa had been with balloons and streamers everywhere and overflowing Santa bags. I used to sew them a costume each year, so they could dress up like a pirate, clown, princess or fairy on Christmas Day. I still feel extremely guilty that I wasn't there for my two kids that year.

Sam and I flew back to Victoria together to spend New Year there. I was in the process of moving to a new place which was near our school and had three bedrooms, so Ruby could have her own room. We could walk to school in five minutes, so it was very convenient.

I had also organised a family reunion during this time at a school camp venue in Port Fairy. Since 1996, Mum's side of the family had held a weekend reunion every year for everyone to come together and catch up, reminisce about Nanna and Poppa, dance our Scottish dances, and play music together. I had found these occasions quite challenging most years and had ended up very worse for wear at many of them. I drank because I felt anxious about being in the family spotlight.

I thought that this would be a good opportunity to introduce Sam to the extended family. We started drinking quite early that day and all headed up to the pub for more drinks. Sam was quite pissed by the time the evening rolled around and was not making a good impression on my family. We were sitting in a circle chatting back at the camp venue and I noticed my brother-in-law getting up and going over to where Sam was sitting. The next thing I knew, punches were flying, and I ran out of the room. I was quite drunk myself and fell asleep in one of the bunk rooms.

When I woke up the next morning I immediately felt a stab of fear. 'Oh my God, what happened last night?' I tentatively left the bedroom and could hear hushed voices talking about the previous night. Mum and Dad had gone to their holiday house because they were really upset, and my aunty came to read me the riot act. I told Sam to take my car and go to my place and stay there.

He had taken quite a few loads of stuff around to my new place by the time the kids and I arrived back. He was also agitated. I was quite scared by his behaviour, to be honest and thought, *Just continue unpacking your stuff and keep it normal.* He went on a rant about the new place having mice and went to buy mouse traps and set them up around the house. Sally called in and she said, 'What the hell is wrong with him?'

In Sydney, I had had my suspicions that he was taking drugs, but now I was convinced that he was. He was paranoid, erratic, sweating, and very jumpy. I kept thinking, *Just be cool and behave normally until he leaves.* I knew that he was seriously bad news by then and kept up my act of normality until I put him on the train back to Melbourne. I felt so relieved watching that train pull away from the station and I never saw Sam again. I didn't answer his calls or return his emails. He wrote a letter apologising to my mum for ruining the family reunion, but there was no way in hell that I was ever going to respond.

Sally and Sandy decided to take me out and cheer me up after this debacle. I wasn't keen and said so. They said, 'Get ready or we will come and drag you out.' I got ready and waited for them, wine in hand on the front porch. Bill was home for a visit and the kids were staying with him for a couple of days. True to our usual form, we went on a pub crawl. Our town nearly has a pub on each corner, so we were half pickled by stop number four.

We decided to visit our old uni days haunt which used to have a reputation as the wildest pub in town, especially over the silly season. The 'Cri' was packed and I lost my friends in the front bar. A guy sitting on a bar stool said, 'Hi, are you looking for me?' or something cheesy like that. I ignored him and went outside to see if they were out there. I couldn't find them, so I decided to walk up to the taxi rank and go home. It was late by this stage, and as I left the pub and was walking up the street, a voice behind me said,

'A lovely lady like you shouldn't be out walking by herself at night. Can I accompany you?' It was the guy who had tried to chat me up from the pub.

I think I was quite rude and said, 'Listen, mate, I don't need any help from you or anyone else.' He didn't take the hint and walked with me to the taxi rank. He was quite tall, with thick, dark hair, and looked like a decent guy.

I had been quite short with him and I introduced myself and he said, 'Keith's the name, would you like to share a taxi with me?'

I said, 'Okay.' I went home, paid my share of the fare, and went inside.

A couple of weeks went by, and school had resumed for the new year. Keith called by out of the blue to ask if I wanted any help around my new place. He seemed very friendly, and we chatted for a while. I was impressed by his friendly and caring manner, and he was easy to talk to. I didn't have a lawnmower and the lawns needed cutting, so he said that he would bring his mower around and cut my lawns. I was grateful and invited him to stay for tea. Ruby did not like him from the minute she saw him. She threw a heat pack at him while he was sitting at the dining room table. I was cross with her and asked her to apologise to Keith. She did so very begrudgingly and did not make life easy for my newest suitor. He wasn't deterred at all, and he started to come around to fix things, occasionally bringing casseroles for our dinner.

I was sharing a class that year with another teacher who was the opposite of me in every way. She was very abrupt, treated me like a student, and I was very intimidated by her. I was so anxious when she was present in the classroom that I couldn't even play my guitar, and that had never happened to me before. Ruby had been in her class the year previously and used to say, 'Mummy, I don't want to go to school.' When I asked her why, she said, 'Ms Jones is grumpy and awful to us.'

I didn't believe her and said, 'All the teachers at our school are very hard working and fair, sweetheart; maybe she was just a bit tired and busy.'

Ruby was correct; if anything, she had played down just how mean and nasty she was. She would correct me in front of the class while I was teaching, disagree with comments I made, observe me working with small groups of students, and then tell me that my questioning and methods needed improvement. I had never experienced being browbeaten in front of a class, made to feel inadequate, and undermined in every way. It was the only time that I ever contacted the Australian Education Union to ask them to intervene. I was very close to breaking point and was drinking heavily every night.

I was extremely anxious and tense all the time and I couldn't turn my neck. I was seeing a sports masseuse on my chiropractor's recommendation and she said that my shoulders were like rocks. I was having awful stress headaches and even coming home from school at lunchtime to lie down for a while. A colleague in the adjoining classroom to me said that I should start keeping a diary of what was transpiring, because he could hear a lot of what was occurring and was concerned too. I started writing down what was happening as evidence that I wasn't going mad. I can recall having to remain at school and teach our class when she was held up at her other 'position', correct pages of work that I didn't set and attend excursions that required me to leave very early so I had to make arrangements for the kids to be looked after. It was the worst year of my teaching career. In hindsight, I should've gone out on stress leave because it was just so awful. Thankfully, the union came through and I was moved into another role in the school, working in the library.

I just drifted into my relationship with Keith; I didn't give it much thought, to be honest. I was so stressed and worn down with school that I needed someone to just be there. He loved to drink as well, so we did become good drinking buddies. It was nice to have another adult to vent to at the end of another awful day.

Keith owned a cottage with an adjoining block of land in Mailors Flat about ten minutes out of town. The cottage was quite small but cute, and I spent a lot of time there helping him to make it cosy and homely. One Friday night, when the kids had gone to Melbourne to see their father, he cooked me a lovely dinner and then got down on one knee and proposed, opening a box which held a stunning emerald ring. I was very flattered that he had remembered that I loved emeralds as this gem is my birthstone.

What could I say? I was totally blown away by the romantic setting; he had placed the table in front of the open fire and beautifully set it with a table cloth, flowers, and a bottle of champagne in an ice bucket. I was half pissed already by then and said, 'Yes, of course.'

My Scottish grandad and
me in 1967

My first night in the band
with the newspaper
clipping from that night

First day of Uni (Sally and me)

Dad and me on my wedding
day in 1983

21st Birthday Pic Sally,
Sandy, and me

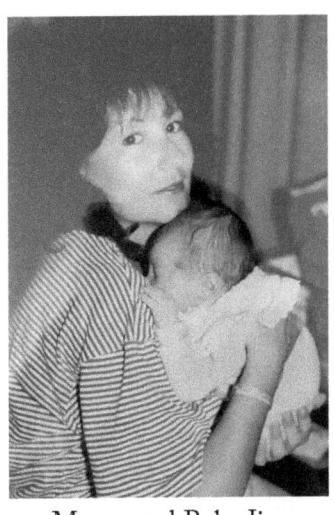

Margy and Baby Jim

Starting on life's carousel, 1968

Margy as Dame Edna, Jim as
a swaggie, and Ruby as Nutsy
Koala on 'Aussie Dress Up
Day' 1998

Viking pic of me taken in
Lerwick, Shetland 2014

Lottie Jackson

Sally and Sandy wearing
the dreaded 'Fantasia'
bridesmaid dresses,
20 August 1983

'The Sparl', Brae,   Margy and Granny
Shetland 1975   Jackson, Kirkcaldy,
Fife 1975

Chapter 12
Remarriage and other bruises
Trigger Warning: Domestic Violence

The kids and I moved out to Keith's cottage on New Year's Eve 2004. I decided to take long service leave for term one 2005 to recuperate after a brutally tough year of teaching, and so I could concentrate on preparing for our wedding in February. So, we organised the whole thing ourselves. The service was held on our spare block of land next to the cottage in a portable gazebo having a marriage celebrant perform the service. I had catered for the reception with antipasto platters, a buffet with hot roast meat and vegetables, and a wedding cake dessert. Jen and Fi came down from Queensland and helped me out again, and we had a terrific celebration.

The reception was held in the Mailors Flat Hall, and the ladies' committee kindly helped with serving and cleaning up. On our way back up the hill walking home, Keith was a bit worse for wear and carried a slab of beer on his shoulder. Allan and my family drove past us, and Allan wound down his window and said, 'Hey mate, that's not Margy on your shoulder; she is right behind you,' laughing his head off. I was stuffed by the time we got home and just wanted to crawl into bed.

I took off the wedding gear and climbed into bed. Unfortunately, I had forgotten to turn off the overhead light and called out, 'Hey hon, can you please turn the light off, so I don't have to get out of bed again?'

He was drunk by this stage and came in, grabbed me by the arms and shook me while growling, 'Don't fucking tell me what to do, ever!'

I was shocked and thought, *Here I go again.*

Keith wasn't working, as he had been on an illness disability for a bad skin condition which caused him terrible itching and rashes. However, he was a handy bloke, and he had attached an annexe to the rear of the cottage so we would have enough room for the four of us.

We had decided to build a new house on the adjacent block because the cottage was far too small for four people. It was a Kentucky Napier home, constructed by a company that built relocatable homes to the builder's specifications. The house was constructed in the builders' yard in town and transported to our block on semi-trailers. I had decided to write a letter to Keith's insurance company, the one attached to his superannuation policy, to see if he could be paid a lump sum instead of the monthly pension. They were open to this idea, so we went ahead and asked for a settlement. I had worked out that if he stayed on the disability pension for the rest of his life, it would work out to be a couple of million dollars. We needed the money to build the house, and the settlement, in the end, was $120,000. We also sub-divided the two blocks and sold the cottage.

The kids were at secondary school by this stage. Jim was very musical and had mastered playing the drums at an early age and was now picking up my guitar and playing it upside down as I am right-handed and he is left-handed. He had played 'Forever Young' by Bob Dylan at the wedding ceremony and had impressed everyone with his stunning performance. He spent a lot of his time in his room writing songs and declared to me one day in the cottage that he had written enough songs for an album.

Ruby had enjoyed being in the chorus of her school musical that year and had a great voice. She decided to audition for the local holiday show for young performers that summer. I think Keith found it challenging to have an instant family. He had never been married and had no children of his own. He had suffered the loss of his father when he was twelve, and his fiancée had died in a car accident when he was in his early twenties. He had never had counselling after his dad died and had left school early as a result. He used alcohol to self-medicate and was not a pleasant drunk. One night, he had driven into town to get some more beer and had been pulled over by the cops. An immediate loss of licence had resulted. He had to get an alcohol interlock device fitted to his car and was suspended from driving for eighteen months. It was his third drink-driving offence. This was the first time I had heard about this, and life was about to get even more challenging.

Building the house was a stressful experience, and every week, the cost increased, and there was another hurdle to jump over. I dealt with the financial side of it as Keith was not good with money, and it seemed just to disappear when he had it. His smoking and drinking habits were costing us about $250 a week. I was also drinking heavily, and I persuaded Keith to start drinking wine because beer was so expensive. I started buying cheap bottled wine, and Keith cut back a bit on his beer. The cheapest bottle of wine was $1.99 a bottle, which was much less than almost $20 for a six-pack of beer. I was extremely worried that we would run out of money before the house was even placed on the block. I drank a lot to cope with everything and just prayed that we would be able to complete the place and move in. It was so important to me to build a new home for my kids after moving them around so much.

I moved mountains trying to get that place finished and realised that I would have to get another job to afford the place, or Keith would have to go back to work. He had started a home business fixing mowers and assorted appliances, but it wasn't enough to cover our mortgage and living costs. Keith was also a person with very little ambition or self-belief. I tried to encourage him by getting a flash sign made to sit out the front of our house and advertise his business. I made flyers and delivered them all over the place and put ads in the local paper. Financially, things were getting desperate. I applied for another job as the education officer at our local entertainment centre. I was successful in obtaining this position and fitted it in around my teaching schedule.

The pressure was really on now, or should I say, again. I was the sole driver with two teenagers who needed transport in and out of town all the time. I quite often made five trips in and out of Warrnambool daily. I had to do all the shopping, messages, and running around and meet the demands of two jobs. I began to think that I had probably been an axe murderer in a past life to incur all the bad luck that I was attracting. I was still drinking, but I had to be very careful of how much when I was required to be everyone's chauffeur. Keith was drinking a lot, and I was beginning to understand that he had a very big alcohol problem. I knew that he liked to drink but wasn't aware that it had escalated to nearly all day, every day. Once again, I tried to keep our home life running smoothly, but the old eggshells were pricking my feet under my Ugg boots once more.

Our house was finally delivered to the block in November 2005. It arrived on three separate semi-trailers and was lifted into place by a crane. There was an upstairs section which had two bedrooms and a bathroom.

The crane swayed a bit lifting this section of the house into place. We watched with bated breath as the house took shape on our block. I was very excited because I felt like I hadn't been home properly since the kids and I had left our lovely place five years before. The neighbours were quite shocked as when they had left for work that morning the block had been empty and coming home there was a new house. The builders took a very long break over the summer period, much to our dismay, and the shell of the house just sat there until late January. I used to go over and sit in the house and try to work out just how we were going to pay for it. By then, the money was almost all gone, so I just kept drinking and worrying.

Jim started playing in a band with his mates from high school. They became very popular and won a Battle of the Bands competition and had regular gigs at several places in town. I was pleased that he had music to soothe him and provide an outlet for his increasing creativity. He spent most of his time ensconced in his tiny bedroom, writing songs and playing my guitar. The music in the house provided me with comfort, as I was very fearful that I had made a terrible mistake in marrying Keith.

We slowly managed to complete the house and moved in at the end of April 2006. We ran next door to the cottage with baskets and boxes, shifting our belongings into the new place. To save money, we painted the interior ourselves and got a painter to do the outside. The house was western red cedar and had to be treated with a thick, treacle-like substance to preserve the wood.

The guy we employed to paint the outside of the house was totally useless. His apprentice painted over windows, left some sections unfinished, and generally did a terrible job. Keith paid the guy in cash before it was completed, much to my dismay. We chased this guy for months to get him to return and complete the job, but he didn't finish it. We finally lodged a complaint with the Victorian Civil and Administrative Tribunal (VCAT) and went to court.

I represented us in court and had everything documented in triplicate and ready to go. The judge asked me to approach the bench after I had presented our case, complete with double copies of quotes, photos of the awful job, transcripts of phone conversations, and a detailed account of what had transpired. She asked, 'Are you a schoolteacher, by any chance?'

I replied, 'Yes, I am,' and she chuckled.

'I thought so; I have *never* seen anyone this prepared before, so I am going to award you full damages.'

We were ecstatic, but the defendant didn't even come to the hearing and had gone bankrupt, so we only got back some of the money owed to us.

All of this had taken its toll on me, and I knew the anxiety and fear were bearing down on me again. Once more, I confided in my wonderful GP and was given time off from work—from two jobs, this time. I was scared and liked everyone to be in the house with me when they were home. The kids comforted me because they knew that my anxiety was extreme, and we watched my favourite movies together. I felt like the whole world was on my shoulders, and I was struggling to cope. Money was very tight, and we just scraped by with the mortgage, food, bills, our alcohol and Keith's cigarette addiction. I knew that I was drinking far too much, but I couldn't moderate any more.

I visited my doc and had a chat with her about my concerns. I didn't divulge how much I was drinking, though. She gave me a referral to get my blood work done and then called me to say that she wanted me to take a test for diabetes as my blood sugar was quite high. I went and had this test, and a week later, she informed me that I had 'prediabetes type 2' and that I needed to lose weight to normalise my blood sugar levels and prevent the disease from becoming more serious. I was about ninety kilos and very unfit with the stresses I had been under for so long. In 2010, I embarked once again on a mission to lose weight and improve my health. I started jogging around the block, and I enjoyed it. Jane is a very fit person, and she encouraged me to train with her and do the annual Surf to Surf Fun Run held in Warrnambool each January. I dropped about twenty kilos and started feeling much better. I also cut down on my drinking and focused on improving my health and fitness. I was proud of myself, and I competed in the Surf to Surf for two consecutive years.

Luckily, I was a thrifty cook and could whip up a meal using limited ingredients. One night, all I had left was some sad-looking veggies and some frozen pastry. I whipped up my vegetarian pasties, and the kids said, 'Wow, Mum, these are delicious; I reckon we should put you on *MasterChef*.' I certainly was standing in the front of the line when God was deciding who would parent my children.

The following week I said to Keith, 'You are going back to work. I can't do this anymore by myself.'

I would be in town, and he would ring me and say, 'Can you get me some smokes, beer, and some Ventolin?' It drove me insane. As a person who had kicked the fags yet again, I hated buying them, but look out if I came home empty-handed. If he had been drinking, he could get very aggressive and scary.

I used to ask the kids when I arrived home, 'Who is here tonight, "normal Keith" or the ogre?' It really was like dealing with two different people. When he was sober, he was a mild-mannered, quiet guy. Once he started drinking, he would become progressively angrier, and his eyes would have a crazy look in them like Jack Nicholson's in *The Shining*. It was a good idea to stay out of his way when he had been drinking.

There were many Saturday afternoons when I could see that he was getting argumentative, and the ogre was starting to appear. I would pick up the phone and dial my brother-in-law's number with the intention of asking him to come and help me, but I always put the phone back on the wall.

I was embarrassed that I had found myself in yet another unhappy relationship and decided that I would just have to make the best of it. I really tried to do that by creating a welcoming home, making sure everyone was well-fed, warm and comfortable. The kids knew that Keith was a volatile drunk, and they too made sure that they avoided him when he was drinking heavily.

One Friday evening, when I arrived home from school I sensed straight away that something was wrong. The kids were inside the house, and they looked anxious. I went out to the shed, and Keith was ranting and raving about something and was also trying to start the chainsaw. I was worried that he would injure himself and told him to put it down. He just kept pulling the cord and muttering to himself. I went back inside the house, and we just stayed together and kept quiet. I was scared and frightened that he would do something stupid. He got out the electric clippers and shaved half his hair off and was just manic. Ruby, Jim, and I sat at the dining room table listening to the chainsaw, and we were scared. We discussed calling the police but thought that that would send him totally over the edge. We huddled together on the couch watching a movie, and, in the end, we decided that our best option was to go to bed and hope that Keith would remain outside. I tossed and turned, listening to AC/DC blaring *Highway to Hell* from his shed; the irony was not lost on me. Once it had gone quiet, I snuck down the stairs to see where Keith was. He was fast asleep on some dog blankets in his shed, snoring his head off. I was relieved that he hadn't come inside and left him there to sleep it off.

I felt like I was trying to balance a scale that kept going out of whack. We were just making ends meet, but Keith kept doing crazy things we couldn't afford, like buying a boat that just sat in the backyard. When I asked, 'Why would you buy a boat when we just can't afford it?' he replied, 'It was a bargain.' I was expected to add that to my list of items to pay for. God. I was stressed!

I would hide my credit card so Keith wouldn't find it, but he always managed to locate it and run up massive debts. He thought nothing of taking out two or three hundred dollars cash at seventeen per cent interest on my credit card and spending it on grog or crap. My stomach was in knots from the stress and, at one point, I really thought the bank would foreclose on our loan after I couldn't pay it for a month. I very reluctantly wrote a letter to my dad, asking him for some money to help us out. He wrote back to me straight away saying he would and that he knew we were under a lot of financial pressure. I was so relieved because it meant that we could remain in our house. I hate asking for *any* help full stop, let alone for money. I am a proud Scottish person, too and this just didn't sit well with me.

I finally convinced Keith that he had to return to work; I couldn't continue keeping the whole ship afloat. A maintenance position was advertised in the local paper with the city council. I wrote the application for him, and he got an interview and then the position. It was such a relief financially and to be able to come home to a husband who hadn't been drinking all day. The first few months were fantastic, and I breathed a huge sigh of relief.

My position at the entertainment centre had run out of funding, so I was able to just concentrate on my teaching role. I had developed a new program called 'The Creatives' for children who were talented in music, drama, and the performing arts. I really enjoyed teaching this group, and it was the highlight of my week at school. The students enjoyed it, too, and frequently spoke about how much confidence and motivation it gave them to pursue the performing arts outside school. I was rapt to hear this because, as a former performer myself, I know that you require a lot of self-belief to stand up in front of an audience. Many of these students went on to act in local productions, create new bands and perform individually, even on television. I keep in touch with quite a few of these talented young people.

Sandy messaged me one day to say, *Guess where I am?* It was Melbourne Cup Day, so I replied, *At the Melbourne Cup?* She explained that she had been admitted to the hospital for tests. She had suffered from chronic asthma for years and hadn't been well for quite a long time. She was teaching at the same school as Jane, so I was worried to hear this news. I went to visit her in hospital and smuggled in a bottle of sav blanc. We had a sneaky tipple and thought it was funny. When I left the hospital that day, I had this sinking feeling in the pit of my stomach. I knew that this was serious and prayed that she would be okay as she had a young daughter and was a single mum by this stage.

She ended up having an operation in Melbourne and having one lung removed. She was able to recuperate at her parents' home, and her lovely family were looking after her. She became more and more frail and unwell and had to carry an oxygen tank around with her. Sally and I visited and tried to lift her flagging spirits, but she knew that she was dying.

We had a seafood night early in 2011 and lots of our old friends from our uni days were there. I got as pissed as a fart and ended up staying the night. The next morning, as I came down the stairs, I saw Sandy sitting quietly in her chair with her eyes closed, just dozing. I had a flashback to canoeing down the Glenelg River in our third year of uni with Sandy berating me because I had forgotten to put the tent in the canoe. She was really pissed off with me, and I said, 'Oh well, at least I remembered to bring the wine cask.'

She looked so small and fragile sitting there with the oxygen mask over her face. I had just returned to the classroom that year after being a specialist teacher for many years, and I was sharing a year four class with another teacher. Sandy had returned to the hospital for a couple of weeks. I had gone to visit her over the weekend, but I was told that only family was allowed into the room. The following Friday morning I was setting up my classroom for the day when the phone rang. It was a mutual friend calling to tell me that Sandy had passed away early that morning. It was like being king hit. I dropped the phone and fell backwards against the wall. My colleague in the other room heard the noise and came rushing in to help me and send my students outside. Keith came to school and drove me home. I sat all day on the couch, feeling numb and drinking wine. Sally came over in the afternoon, and we both just cried and sat there together holding hands and looking at old photo albums. It was one of the saddest days of my life.

Sandy's funeral was held in March, and I went on a week-long bender. I don't remember much about this time other than I hid in a wine bottle and grieved for my friend. I had even forgotten to pick up Sally on the way to the funeral, and she was very upset with me. I had been asked to sing at the funeral service, but I was so upset I just couldn't do it.

Sandy's death had also coincided with Jim moving to Melbourne for his music career. By this stage, he was extremely sick of Keith's drunken behaviour, as he had been quite aggressive towards Jim several times. In recent conversations, Jim said that Keith seemed to just switch from being quite normal to becoming totally psychotic. Jim is a sensitive and caring young man, and he struggled to live with Keith. I feel so guilty about making him live in such a toxic environment.

Ruby was in Year Twelve and working very hard in her chosen subjects. She had been the lead actor in a summer production, and it was fantastic to see her doing what she loved to do. This also gave her respite from the daily arguments and the toxic atmosphere at home.

Over the summer holidays, Keith had gotten very drunk one night. He was making a fuss about where I had placed the milk in the fridge. It was really that petty. 'Why do you move things all the fucking time? You just try and confuse me and hide stuff.' I tried to be calm and placate him; this was common behaviour when he was drunk. I did my best to stay out of his way, but he kept badgering me and getting quite aggressive. I could see the ogre starting to appear and went upstairs to our bedroom. Keith followed me, stomping up the stairs and cursing under his breath. I told him to just go outside and calm down. He continued ranting and raving and grabbed me, slapped me across the face, and threw me onto the floor. I went into the bathroom, and I locked the door. Keith went back to his shed, and I waited for a while and then went to bed. I was startled to wake up and see a policeman standing at the foot of my bed. I thought that I was dreaming for a minute. No, there was really a policeman standing at the foot of my bed. I sat up abruptly, and he asked me if I was okay. I told him that I was fine and that I had been sleeping. I went on to say to him, 'The only time I have ever had anything to do with the police before this is when you guys come to school to talk to my students about stranger danger and road safety.' He was very polite and explained that Keith had called the police and they had to come out to Mailors Flat to make sure that everything was alright.

Ruby told me that she heard Keith on the phone to the police, drunkenly telling them that I was aggressive towards him. They came out to our property and went to find Keith in his shed. Ruby said that she heard Keith say, 'Get 'em, Sally' (he was coaxing his red heeler dog to attack the cops). Sally was the most placid and sweet-natured dog you could ever meet. The police sprayed Keith with pepper spray and took him into custody. This resulted in us going to court and the judge advising him to stay two hundred metres away from our house if he had been drinking. He really pulled his head in after this, because I had started looking for a place to rent in town. Ruby and I drove around during the holidays, but there was nothing suitable, and I didn't want to unsettle her before her final year at secondary school.

I had to attend counselling for women affected by domestic violence at Emma House, and I always felt embarrassed and ashamed that I had ended up in this situation. The sympathetic counsellor told me that it didn't matter what your socio-economic background was or how educated you are; domestic violence didn't discriminate. Ruby was also supposed to attend this counselling, but she was very focused on her studies and wasn't keen to go. I understood how difficult this was for her, and I didn't push her to attend counselling. I had protected her several times when Keith was in a bad temper.

Ruby stood up to him one night, and he went to grab her. I stood in front of her and told her to walk back up the stairs while saying to Keith, 'If you lay one hand on my daughter you will never see me ever again.' He never touched Ruby, but I was very anxious that he might get really drunk and harm her.

I had an elderly great-uncle who lived in Mackay in Queensland and Mum wanted to go and see him. Mum, Dad, Jane, Allan, and I all went. Ruby stayed behind because she had just started Year Twelve, and I hoped that she would be okay with Keith at home for a couple of days. I did go next door and speak discreetly to my next-door neighbour, who was a social worker, and I asked her if she would just keep a look out for Ruby while I was away. I gave her my mobile phone number, and she was very cooperative and gave me hers as well. I left to go to Mackay feeling quite confident that Ruby would be safe.

It was nice spending time with my immediate family, and just the five of us being together evoked memories of our trip to Scotland in 1975. I was also catching up with Elizabeth from high school, who I hadn't seen for many years. She was the girl I used to smoke in the toilets with. I had become a Facebook user, and one day her name popped up on my feed. I messaged her and said, *Hello stranger, what have you been up to for the past thirty-odd years?* She responded by saying that she was a district nurse and lived near Mackay in Queensland. I replied, *What a coincidence, I have an elderly aunt and uncle who live near Mackay,* and told her their names. She disappeared for a minute and then said, *You won't believe this, but I am their visiting nurse.* They do say that life is stranger than fiction. So, she was coming to my great-uncle's house to see my family and me while we were staying in Mackay. It was so surreal to see her again after so many years.

'You haven't changed a bit since high school,' I said. She laughed in her very gravelly, distinctive way, and we hugged. I had organised to spend a night at her place just outside Mackay, and my family were fine with that. Wow, did we have a lot to talk about! Sandy had been a good friend of hers, too, and she had been unable to come down to Victoria for the funeral. I filled her in on her illness and everything that had happened. We basically talked and drank all night. It was so incredible to see her again as I had thought of her many times over the years; she was a hoot.

We were sitting at the airport waiting for our flight home when a tropical storm blew in. The plane was delayed for a couple of hours, so I rang Keith to let him know I would be late home. He sounded drunk on the phone, and I was worried about Ruby. I had spoken briefly to her earlier in the day, and she was fine. I just hoped that she would stay out of Keith's way. I also called my next-door neighbour and explained that Keith was drinking, and could she pop over and check to see if Ruby was alright. She did this, and I was very glad that I had taken the time to speak with her before I had gone on the trip. It was a long flight back and then a long drive home from Melbourne. By the time I got home, I was beside myself with worry. Keith was snoring his head off in bed, and Ruby was okay, thank God! It was so difficult to keep these things secret from my family, and if they knew what was going on, I am sure they would've made us leave.

Not long after this, I went to Melbourne to see Jim early in the year, and we had a terrific weekend. I had missed the afternoon train home and had to catch the later train. I knew that I would have to 'pay' for my lovely time with Jim. By the time I got home, the ogre was in full flight, cursing and yelling and frightening the crap out of me. He was totally out of control and punched his hand into the wall outside our bedroom. He then punched me, grabbed me, and threw me up against the bedroom wall. After he left our bedroom, I went and lay on the bathroom floor, clutching my stomach. I went to bed very upset and tried to sleep, because I had to go to school the next day.

It was a really hot day, and I was wearing long sleeves to hide my bruised arms. I had sore breasts, too, as he had grabbed them and twisted them. A colleague of mine said, 'Why don't you take off your cardigan? It is boiling today.' I pulled him aside later and showed him my bruised arms. He was totally gobsmacked and said, 'Do you want me to come and sort him out for you?' I said that I would deal with it in my own way. Looking back on this time now, I regret not asking for help. My shame and pride kept me from reaching out, and I realise now that I could've easily been another domestic violence statistic.

This whole year was a nightmare, and I do not know how Ruby achieved the excellent results she did to become the female dux of her year. I cheered with pride when her name was called out, and she walked up to the dais to collect the cup. Ruby had received a perfect score for her voice studies and sang a solo at the final assembly; you could have heard a pin drop. She was brilliant. At school the following day, I overheard another teacher saying, 'I went to the Brauer College final assembly last night, and this tiny little girl got up and sang that song by Kate Bush, 'Wuthering Heights'. She was one of the most incredible singers that I have ever heard.' I smiled to myself in the knowledge that Keith's violent behaviour hadn't spoilt Ruby achieving top marks and receiving such well-deserved praise.

Ruby went off to uni in 2012. We drove her up to Ballarat with all her gear and helped her to move into a central apartment with a couple of her friends from home. She was so excited to be starting this new chapter of her life and to be leaving behind a very stressful home environment.

I shed quite a few tears on our journey home, and I thought to myself, *If Keith and I can't make this work now, we are stuffed.* It was very strange not having my gorgeous girl to look after. I used to watch her from the decking outside my bedroom, walking down the road in the morning with her bag slung over her back, to get on the school bus. Every time I hear the Abba song, 'Slipping Through My Fingers', I cry. I loved being a mum and taking care of my kids. Life just wasn't the same with only Keith and I at home. He continued to spend most of his time in the shed drinking and smoking, and I stayed in the house cooking and watching TV, wine glass firmly in hand. You can be very alone in a relationship, and I felt very alone that year.

Jim had made a couple of EPs by then and had been touring around Australia with the singer/songwriter Josh Pyke. Josh had been mentoring Jim, and the two of them got on well. They were doing a gig in Brisbane, and Jen and Fi were very keen to go and see the show. Ruby and I flew up and stayed with Fi and Phil in Brisbane for several days. We all went to see Jim play and they were so proud of their 'boy' and his success. It was a wonderful few days catching up with my friends and their families. Again, I had the feeling that we had been destined to meet because our relationship was so special to me. I always cry my eyes out when we have to part, and this time was no different.

Waiting at the Brisbane airport to fly home, Ruby said, 'Mum, I am really worried about you living with Keith. I know that you have just accepted it as your lot, but I am scared that one day I will get a call saying that he has hurt you and put you in hospital.' I tried to reassure her that things were okay, but I sensed that they were escalating, and the violent outbursts were becoming more frequent.

She went on to say that I needed to tell the family what was happening so that they could help me and that if I wouldn't tell them, she was going to. I have only realised recently that Ruby had thought this through very carefully, and she knows me so well that there is no way I would've let her tell the family. I realised at that point I had no option but to speak with my family and let them know the truth. I organised a coffee catch-up for the following week and sat down with Mum and Jane and told them that things weren't good at home. They were very supportive, and it was a relief to share my worry with them. I decided to start looking for a place in town, and I attended several viewings over the next few weeks. There was one place that I liked in central Warrnambool, and the agent said that it would be available after Christmas. I made the decision to lease the property and signed the tenancy forms.

This unit in town was clean and modern. It was just around the corner from Mum and Dad. Mum had come around the day I looked at it and been a hit with the real estate agent because she was dressed as an elf. It was a week before Christmas, and the choir she was in had been performing at a Christmas function. I joked with her that the only reason I was the successful applicant was that she had hugged everyone dressed like Santa's helper. The unit was very central, so I could walk into town easily. The bottle shop was just up the road, too, which was very handy.

All I had to do was navigate the week or so until Christmas, and then I could leave my violent, obnoxious, alcoholic husband. I went about my report-writing and end-of-year activities at school feeling relieved that I had finally made the decision to end this hell on earth.

*

Aussie teachers have it tough, I reckon! The end of our school year also coincides with Christmas and the silly season. Every year there are reports to write, end-of-year assemblies, carols, performances, the staff Christmas party, and then you think, *Crap, it is Christmas next week.* The end of 2012 was no exception.

It had been a hot day at school; the kids were tired, cranky, and fed up. I got home looking forward to just sitting in the air-conditioned lounge room and relaxing. Keith came in and asked, 'Can you run me into town to my Christmas party?'

I was stuffed but said, 'Okay, if you can get ready soon, I will take you back into town.' After about twenty minutes, I went and sat in the car to take him into town. I turned on the ignition to cool the car down—still no Keith. I got out of the car and went to the shed to find him standing there having smoke and a stubby. I was getting a bit cranky by this stage, and I just wanted to have a rest. 'Can you get a move on please? I have been in the car waiting for you.' I could tell that he had already sunk a few beers because his eyes had their 'crazy' look, and he was slurring his words.

Eventually, he got in the car and, by then, I wasn't in a good mood. We went down our lane and pulled onto the main road. 'What's up your arse?' he asked gruffly.

I was so worn out and tired by then I said, 'You have kept me waiting in the car for nearly half an hour, I am tired, and I just want to stop and have a rest,' as a tear slid down my face.

He said, 'You are always fucking tired or cross. You can get fucked.' He reached over and pulled the handbrake on.

The car skidded across the main road. I was terrified and tried to steer the car so it wouldn't hit the gravel. If there had been a car on the other side of the road, we would've had a head-on collision. I corrected the car and kept driving. My hands were shaking uncontrollably. Tears were pouring down my face. I took him to the party venue, and he got out and thumped his fist on the bonnet. I just hoped that he would rub someone else up the wrong way, and he would get what he deserved. I thought I would just keep driving up to Melbourne to stay with Jim. I realised that I was too upset and tired to drive, so I went home. I thought, *Just have a rest and a sleep and if you still feel this upset, then leave tomorrow morning.*

I usually made pizza on Friday nights, but I decided to go and get a pizza from Bojangles on my way home. While I was waiting, a colleague from school saw me. It was her birthday, and she was going out for dinner to celebrate. I remember her looking at me strangely and asking me if I was alright. I instinctively knew that she had seen the despair on my face, but I was still trying to save face and pretend that I was okay.

Keith didn't come inside the house to sleep that night, thank goodness. I got up in the morning, packed my bag and went to the car.

'Where the fuck are you going?' he growled at me.

I replied, 'As far away from you as I can possibly get.'

I stopped for lunch on the way to my destination and went into a store to buy a pie. As usual, Keith had taken every cent from my wallet, and I actually grinned, thinking, *This is the last time you will ever do this to me.* I drove to Apollo Bay and stayed there for the weekend. When I returned home, I went to tell my family what had happened. They were horrified, and they wanted me to move out straight away. I stayed for another week in Jim's room downstairs. The night before I left for good, Ruby asked, 'Aren't you going to start packing, Mum?' I had not moved one thing because I instinctively knew that this would just send Keith into a total meltdown. So, on the morning I departed, the house looked the same as it always had; even the Christmas tree lights were still twinkling away. I asked Keith to not be present when I was moving out, and he went off in his Land Cruiser ute for the day.

I hired a large van, and my wonderful family all came and removed my things. It looked very bare by the time we finished. We took my belongings around to the new unit and set everything up. It was just so weird waking up in my own home that morning and then being transplanted into totally new surroundings. I was feeling very unwell and shaky. I walked up to the bottle shop, got some wine, and drank myself into a stupor. I was awoken by the phone ringing. It was the cops. They wanted to make sure that I was okay and not hiding in the house. Keith had gone on a wild rampage, and our neighbours had called them after hearing loud banging coming from the house.

I assured them that I was fine, and then I called Keith's brother to let them know what had happened.

I wasn't feeling well at the start of 2013. My anxiety had increased with my heavy drinking, and I was quite alone and scared. I had a lovely elderly next-door neighbour who would check in on me and have a chat quite regularly. I spent New Year's Eve at her place, crying into my wine glass.

Call 1800RESPECT if you or anyone you know is experiencing domestic violence.

Chapter 13
Green monsters and red wine

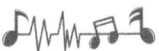

Mum, Dad, Jane, Allan, and I made another trip up to Mackay to see my great uncle in March 2013. I had only been in my unit for a couple of months, and I was struggling being by myself and feeling displaced. I had been out several times at home and dated some very unsuitable men. I had really given up on myself and didn't care what happened to me. The kids were both busy with their own lives in Melbourne, and I felt like I was not needed.

On the trip to Mackay, I said to Allan, 'I hate being on my own.'

He thought I was mental, as he and his wife had a two-year-old, and their life was hectic. He said, 'I would give anything for some time by myself.'

Isn't it strange in life how we often pine for things we can't have when, at other times, we want the opposite?

Jim was doing well with his performing career, and he and his band 'The Triple Threat' had been chosen as the support act for the American band Counting Crows. They were playing at the Sydney Opera House in early April, and I decided to go. I invited a couple of friends, Terri and Toni, to come with me. Terri had been the wife of a bass player in one of our bands, and we had also been at uni at the same time. Toni was a friend from my uni days too; her former partner had been one of Bill's good mates, and we had stayed friends. I had booked a nice apartment in Darling Harbour, and we played tourists for a couple of days.

The morning after we arrived in Sydney, we caught the monorail into the city and went shopping. We stopped in a lovely old arcade and found a clothing store having a sale. There was a jacket that I liked, and Toni suggested that I should try it on. I did, but it was a bit too tight. I had put on weight throughout the stresses of the past year or so, and I was a bit embarrassed about it. She kept on and on, saying, 'You should still buy it; you will lose the weight.'

I just wanted her to stop, so I said, with some exasperation, 'Please stop saying that, or I will punch you one.'

The mood totally went downhill after that. We went for a coffee, and she wouldn't even look at me, much less reply to anything I said. We were going on the bus to Bondi, and they sat apart from me. I attempted to apologise, but she was not even going to acknowledge me.

I went back into the city by myself to have lunch with Jim because it was his birthday. I went with him to the soundcheck for the evening's performance. I was sitting with the girlfriends of the guys in Jim's band. I asked one of them jokingly, 'Is Jim being a diva?'

She responded by saying, 'Jim is an absolute sweetheart. He went and got everyone a coffee without anyone asking him to. He was so concerned about making sure that everyone is feeling okay and not too nervous.' One very proud mum went back to the apartment to get ready that afternoon!

Toni and Terri came back later in the afternoon, and we all got ready to go to the Opera House. The record company had provided drinks and nibbles for us in the Aria Bar before the show. It should have been a great night, but the tension was awful. Jim's recording company executives were there, and Toni harped on about her children and their achievements when I was trying to chat to them about Jim. I was so disappointed that such an incredible experience of seeing my son play at the Opera House was totally ruined.

Jim and his band were fantastic, I have never been prouder of him in my life. To see him performing on stage at the Sydney Opera House was like a dream. He was confident, he owned the stage, and the audience loved him. I was the proudest mum in Australia that night. The applause at the end was amazing, and I had tears of pride running unashamedly down my face.

Toni wasn't having a bar of it, though and wanted to leave as soon as Counting Crows were finished. We went back to our apartment in a taxi in silence and went to bed. The next morning, I went out to the lounge area, and Toni appeared and totally did her block at me. I have never been spoken to or been victimised like that ever before, even in my worst Keith bollocking. She called me everything under the sun, from a princess to the town drunk, and she said that everyone was laughing at me behind my back. 'Shit, I don't know what happened to you, the rest of your family are nice people. You will never find a good bloke because you are hopeless.' It was brutal!

Terri appeared in her dressing gown about halfway through Toni's venomous spiel and sat on the couch. I kept glancing over at her, hoping that she would come to my defence. She eventually said, 'Hey, this is getting out of control; just stop, please, Toni.'

It took every ounce of my self-control not to lash out and hit her. I kept my arms pinned by my sides and stood there and took it. I felt like I was in a boxing ring going ten rounds with Mike Tyson.

We flew back to Melbourne the following day. Terri had driven us up to Melbourne in her car and left it at Tullamarine in the car park. Toni did not speak to me again the whole way home. That car trip back from Melbourne was toxic; you could've cut the atmosphere with a knife. I was sitting in the back seat, and I had never felt so invisible in my life. Toni and Terri chatted all the way home, and I just wanted the trip to end. In hindsight, Toni's anger and loathing toward me must have begun a long time before this trip. Jane used to say to me, 'Make sure that you never get on the wrong side of her; I think she is very jealous of you.' When I arrived home late that night, I drank a bottle of red wine and threw up all over the bathroom floor. This horrible experience plunged me further into depression, and my drinking was the worst it had ever been. I was going to school hungover, feeling sick all the time and unable to concentrate on anything. I went to bed, I got up and went to school, I came home and started drinking, and did it all over again. I was as low as I had ever been in my life.

The sense of displacement was overwhelming, and I was drinking far too much. I just wanted to drown everything out and become invisible. I got addicted to an online music game called *SongPop* and was very good at it. I made some new friends playing this game, and we even met up in Melbourne for lunch one day when I was visiting the kids. Ruby was at uni in Melbourne by this time, so now both the kids were living in the 'big smoke', and I went up to see them quite a bit.

On my fiftieth birthday, Ruby met me at Southern Cross Station with a huge bunch of roses in her hand. Then both the kids took me to the Monet exhibition at the National Gallery of Victoria. I was rapt to see the real paintings of Monet's flowers, as one of these has been hanging above my bed for thirty years. We went to The Barre at the Melbourne Arts Centre for champagne and nibbles. Jim was playing a gig that night in the city. I had fun getting lots of hugs from handsome strangers when he told the audience, 'My lovely mum is here tonight, and it is her fiftieth birthday, so go and give her a birthday hug.' I had a wonderful time.

I used my gift voucher from the kids and bought a nice pair of winter boots. I was a bit hungover that day after my big night out celebrating in Melbourne and snoozed all the way home on the lunchtime train.

School was hard. The other teacher with whom I shared a class had a very different teaching style to me, and she said once, 'I think you should try to teach more like me.' I found this quite insulting and impossible. Everyone has their own unique way of teaching, and although I often put a creative spin on boring topics and bent the rules, I cared for every child that came into my class.

Teaching is a job that goes beyond reading, writing, and numeracy. I genuinely cared about my students and spent a lot of time following up on any concerns I had for their welfare. Towards the end of my career, I was spending as much time on planning and teaching as I was on following up concerns about children with the appropriate service providers. This was very stressful and heartbreaking as many more children were presenting with issues like neglect or the physical and emotional results of domestic violence.

We had an Aboriginal educator start at our school. She came in to talk to my class one afternoon. I sat spellbound, listening to her stories of children being taken from their homes and families and the horrendous massacres that had occurred when the Europeans had taken land from our Indigenous people. I was crying at my desk because I am the biggest sook in the world. One of my students noticed and told our visitor. She came over, and we hugged, and one of the kids took a picture. That was a lesson that I will never forget.

The strange, displaced year continued. I did a lot of walking and thinking. One blustery winter's day, I was sitting on the main beach looking at the sea, waves crashing against the windswept coastline. I was low and very sad and thought about just standing up and walking straight ahead into the sea.

My aunty, Dad's youngest sister, had committed suicide like this twenty-five years before in Scotland. She had also suffered greatly from depression and alcoholism. I had always been scared that the same fate might await me because our stories were very similar. It happened to be 20 August 2013, the anniversary of the day Bill and I had married thirty years before. I had taken a walk with Dad and Jane to this exact spot on the morning of the wedding.

If I had been able to see into the future back in 1983, I would never have foreseen myself sitting here on the beach, contemplating my suicide thirty years later. I thought, *I know you think that your life is over and you are giving up hope; just stop and think about your family for a minute. They have been on this crazy journey with you too, and Jim and Ruby don't deserve any more hardship.* I was at the water's edge by then and made myself turn around, and I walked back up the beach.

For anyone experiencing personal difficulties, please call:
Lifeline Australia: 13 11 14
Beyond Blue Australia: 1300 224 636
Suicide Call Back Service: 1300 659 467
Domestic Violence Australia: 1800 737 732 (1800 RESPECT).

Chapter 14
'You can't run away from yourself, Mum'

Meanwhile, Keith was still living in our house. There was no alternative but to sell it, and he was not keen on that idea. I had been out there a couple of times to get things, and the place was dirty, messy, and the walls had been damaged. So I organised a meeting at the bank, and we met there to discuss the loan repayments and how we could keep the mortgage viable until the house was sold. Unfortunately, Keith acted like a total prick in this meeting, and I ended up walking out.

We managed to get a real estate agent to sell our property, but this, too, was a nightmare. I would go out and clean the place when a prospective buyer was going to look through it, and Keith would mess it up. I had taken a day from my long service leave to go and get the place ready for an open house viewing the following day, a Saturday. It took me all day to clean the bathrooms, wash the dirty architraves and floorboards, wipe the muck off the kitchen cupboards and benchtop and make sure it looked nice.

I arrived early on that Saturday morning in July, and he had trashed it again. In tears, I rang Jane and asked her to help me clean it before anyone arrived. We went like the clappers, and Keith dared to come in and say that he was going to 'top himself' before anyone would take his house. Jane finally saw firsthand what I had been dealing with for years.

A young couple were very keen on the house. They put in an offer in September 2013, and we accepted it. Strangely, the young lass was a former student, and I thought it was comforting that a nice person would be living in my much-loved house. I was so relieved when it finally sold. Before the settlement date, I went out and cleaned it once again, but they couldn't move in because Keith hadn't taken his stuff out of the shed.

I started seeing a new therapist in October to work through the aftermath of yet another failed marriage and my feelings about moving forward. I told her that I had kept diaries for years and had poured my heart out in them when times were tough. Her advice was to get rid of them as a symbol of letting go of the past. I understood her reasoning behind this, but I couldn't bear to throw away those journals. At many points in my life, they had been my only way to express my feelings and make sense of what was happening to me. I am so glad I didn't throw them away.

I had to have a break. My whole life had imploded, and I just had to go away for a while. I found out that I could obtain a British passport and went through the rigmarole of doing that. It was an extensive process. I was considering staying in the UK and working there for a while. So I packed up my unit, and Elizabeth, my old 'smoking buddy' from high school, who had moved back home from Queensland, let me store all my furniture and belongings in her shed.

I had been for a mammogram just before Christmas, and I got a call asking me to come in for an ultrasound. I did this, and they found a mass in my right breast, so they wanted to do a biopsy. I was freaked out by this and explained that I was leaving for the UK in early January 2014. The results of the biopsy wouldn't be available until after I arrived in London. I decided to still go, and if the news was bad, I would live it up for a couple of weeks and come home. If the news was good, I would continue with my trip as planned.

Jim, Ruby, and Will, Ruby's partner, saw me off at Tullamarine. I was scared about leaving, but I knew I had to have a break away from everything. Jim hugged me and whispered in my ear, 'You do know that you can't run away from yourself, Mum?' Then, as I walked through the departure gate, I turned to look at my precious children before the automatic doors closed. I still have that image of them smiling together, arm in arm, imprinted in my mind.

The flight to London was very long and very tiring. I had scored a window seat, though, and the seat next to me was empty. I was rapt that I had more space to move. About halfway into the flight, the air hostess came and said, 'There is a guy up the front who has never had a window seat before; he was wondering if you would like to swap seats?' I thought, *'Up the front' meant in business class or better*, so I agreed. It turned out that it was the middle of the front row of economy, right behind the row of bassinets attached to the wall. The rest of the journey was not fun, to say the least, while I listened to crying babies and worn-out parents. I hoped that the guy I had swapped with was now listening to the most boring life story imaginable with chronic diarrhoea!

Arriving in London on a cold, bleak Thursday afternoon in early January 2014 was strange. It was only about half past three, and it was already getting dark. The round, black London cabs had their lights on, and now I had to find my way to where I was staying. I caught the underground after asking for directions and was told to get off at Tower Hill Station. I had a giggle because there is a Tower Hill not far from Warrnambool. I was trying to lug my enormous pink suitcase up the steps when a friendly guy said, 'Let me help you with that.' I was impressed with the manners I had been shown already, as the guy at Heathrow had taken me to the platform where the train left for the city. I got off at Tower Hill and wondered why there were so many people just standing by a wall looking out. It was the Tower of London stop, and they were all admiring the lit-up facade of this famous building.

I wheeled my case out of the station and decided to use the maps feature on my phone to find my apartment, but there was no signal. I was tired and hungry and just wanted to lie down. I went into the nearest pub—there were many pubs—and asked the bartender if he knew where my accommodation was. A guy leaning up at the bar said, 'That is on my way home; you can follow me.' So, off we went, me with my bright pink suitcase, weaving in and out of tiny alleyways, the windows of quaint buildings all fogged up. It was very icy and cold, and people were rushing by with their scarves pulled up over their faces, and I had the weirdest feeling that I had landed in a Charles Dickens novel.

The bloke leading me was in front, and I bloody hoped that he was a decent person, because I didn't want to get mugged or murdered on my first day in London. When he stopped abruptly, I nearly crashed into him. He pointed across the road and said, 'There it is ma'am.' I thanked him profusely, and he nodded and kept walking home.

Phew! I made my way into the foyer, got my key and went up to my well-appointed and very clean apartment, with a comfortable looking bed. It was a huge improvement on the tiny box room that Bill and I had stayed in at Earls Court in 1988. There was even a bath *and* shower in an actual bathroom. I had my laptop with me and checked my emails. My lovely doctor sent a message to say that the biopsy had come back benign, and the tissue mass was a fibroid cyst. I was so relieved I cried. Maybe the black dog had finally stopped following me?

I had a wonderful time in London by myself. On the first morning, I walked back to the Tower of London and had breakfast in the cafe out the front. I spent ages looking around the tower and was blown away when I saw the exact spot where Anne Boleyn had been beheaded. I had just finished watching *The Tudors* miniseries, and to see the real-life locations was amazing. I had wanted to visit the Tower of London with Bill in 1988, but he'd said, 'It's just a touristy place, a bloody rip-off.'

I decided on this visit that I would see everything I had missed seeing back then. So, I waited at the bus stop for a double-decker bus and asked the lady standing next to me if this was the right bus to go to Trafalgar Square. She informed me that, 'It most certainly was,' and we chatted for a while. She turned out to be an ex-teacher herself and said that she went into London every Thursday for the past ten years and did something different. I told her that I had 'Buckley's' of seeing very much in three days, then. She invited me to sit with her on the top deck of the bus and gave me a running commentary of all the sights on the way. We got off at Trafalgar Square, and she asked me in her very British accent, 'Would you care to join me for a spot of tea?' I felt like I had just arrived on the set of Mary Poppins, and I replied, 'I would be delighted to join you.' I felt very posh sitting there with my very proper English friend, holding my teacup and chatting. I even stuck out my pinkie finger as I was drinking my tea. I thanked her profusely for her kindness to a total stranger and went on my way.

Next, I wanted to see Buckingham Palace. My new friend had told me to go through the old stone gate and down the wide street. So off I went, and I was just passing Kensington Palace when a lady rushed past me, frantically pushing a pram. She looked strangely familiar and had her dark hair in a baseball cap with a ponytail out the back. Then some guys on walkie talkies came past as well. The penny dropped! It was the Duchess of Cambridge and baby George. I fumbled to get my phone out to take a pic, but the guards had surrounded her by then. *Wow!* I had just seen on the news that morning that William and Kate had moved into Kensington Palace. I had my own theory that Kate had got fed up being holed up in the palace and wanted to get out for a walk, so she snuck out the back and didn't tell security. The security guys did not look very happy when I had walked past, so I think she had been trying to 'do a runner'! Buckingham Palace is so familiar that it seems strange when you are standing in front of it. It was very cold and drizzly, so there weren't many tourists that day and I got some excellent pics. I decided to return before I left to see the changing of the guard.

I had bought myself a ticket to go and see *Les Misérables* at the Queen's Theatre. It had just opened when I was last here with Bill, and we did queue up outside for tickets. A Cockney scalper said to me, 'Fuck off back to Van Diemen's Land where you belong, ya bloody convicts,' when he heard me telling the young girl behind me that he was charging her much more for her ticket than he was going to charge me. I was very upset about being spoken to like this, so we walked off and found a pub and got drunk.

Coming up out of the underground into the West End of London was incredible. I paused at the underground exit in awe as every show you could think of was on. I thought about how much I wished Ruby was here to share this experience with me, as she was such an avid lover of theatre and musicals. The Queen's Theatre had a huge banner across the front saying, *The 25th Anniversary Show*. I stood there thinking that the last time I was here in this spot was in 1988 when the show had just commenced, and I burst into tears. I love *Les Mis*, and I have seen it several times in Melbourne. The show was brilliant. I sat next to a girl who was also there by herself, and we had a bubbly together during the intermission. At the end, we both just looked at each other, tears streaming down our faces, and bawled into our scarves. I felt that my trip had already been worth it just to see this performance.

I was overwhelmed by the crowds of people, and I felt very alone. It was a strange thought to be anonymous in a city with over nine million people. Australia's whole population is twenty-five million people, which demonstrates just how crowded London is. On my way home from the theatre on the underground, we were packed in like sardines. I was holding onto the coat of a little girl beside me because she was just next to the automatic door, and I was worried that she would fall out when the door opened. Her granny was with her and nodded at me and smiled.

After spending three days in London, I headed off for a quick visit with the English rellies in Slough and Oxford. My cousin in Slough took me to the Warner Brothers' *Harry Potter* studio, where the movies were filmed. I was so excited, being a huge Harry Potter fan, and it was a magical experience. I delighted in seeing the costumes worn by the actors in the movies, all the sets, especially Diagon Alley, the Weasleys' house and the Hogwarts dining hall. I cried when I saw the scale model of Hogwarts, presented in a separate viewing room with the lighting simulating the changing of the seasons. It was simply breathtaking.

I left Manchester Airport to catch a flight up to Scotland. As the plane descended into Glasgow Airport, I was in tears again, thinking that it had been twenty-five years since I had stood on Scottish soil. The lady sitting beside me on the plane gave me a tissue as I wiped my eyes with my sleeve. I went for a cuppa in the cafe, and the young guy behind the counter said, 'Welcome tae bonnie Scotland,' in his broad Scottish accent. He was so welcoming and warm that I burst into tears again, and he came around and hugged me. What a lovely young man. His name was Dylan, and we had our photo taken together after I told him that this was my first visit back to Scotland in twenty-five years. He also refused payment for my cuppa and sandwich. By this stage, I was feeling overwhelmed by the kindness I had been shown by complete strangers. It had restored my faith in human nature.

I flew from Glasgow to Sumburgh in Shetland. The weather was abysmal, and the small plane was rocking from side to side. I could see the wild ocean crashing into jagged rocks from the window of the plane as the plane approached the runway over the stark and treeless, rugged landscape. I prayed to the powers that be to let us land in one piece. My second cousin Catherine and her hubby, Rob, were there to meet me. They had only just been out to Oz in 2011 to help us celebrate Mum and Dad's fiftieth wedding anniversary, but it was wonderful to see them. As we made our way to the car, the wind nearly blew me over, and I recalled that on the previous trip in 1988, Bill and I had to remain for an extra two days because the weather was too wild for the ferry to sail. I call Catherine and Rob my 'Shetland Mam and Da'. Da had cooked a big roast mutton to welcome me, and it was delicious. I was just so thrilled to be in Shetland again. I had consumed a couple of vodkas from my duty-free purchases and then had quite a bit too much wine to drink with my dinner. I think Catherine was fairly concerned when I staggered up the stairs at the end of the evening. I resolved to be a much more well-behaved guest for the remainder of my stay. Catherine and Rob were the most gracious hosts. I was treated like royalty, and I am sure I put on at least a stone of weight eating all the delicious meals that Mam made.

The following day Brenda came to pick me up, and we hugged ourselves silly, and I cried as usual. We talked non-stop for hours and tried to fill each other in on the happenings of the past twenty-five years. I jokingly said to Brenda, 'What would you have said if I told you last time I was here that the next time you see me in real life we will be able to talk to and see each other on our computers and phones in real-time through an invention called the internet?'

She laughed and said, 'I would've thought that you had really lost your marbles.'

Since the last time we had seen each other, technology had come a long way; we had both had two children, and they were in their twenties.

Ever since I was a child, I had heard of the Up Helly Aa festival, held on the last Tuesday of January in Lerwick. Lerwick is the capital of Shetland and is a quaint and historic town with cobblestone streets and small alleyways winding throughout the small town centre. Lerwick is the main harbour in Shetland, and the daily ferry from the mainland departs here to take passengers to Aberdeen in Scotland.

Up Helly Aa, in Lerwick, is the main 'fire festival' which celebrates Shetland's Viking heritage. There are other smaller festivals held in many other villages and towns throughout Shetland. The fire festivals involve a Viking galley boat being built in painstaking detail and then burned after a parade through the town. A group of men are selected to be the Vikings or 'Jarl Squad', and a Viking Chief is chosen; he is called the 'Guiser Jarl'. They dress in full Viking costume, grow their hair and beards long and even get shields and swords made. The detail is quite intricate, and the sight of twenty Vikings storming down the main street was quite terrifying.

This is a very big deal in Shetland and can only be compared in importance to our AFL Grand Final in Victoria. I had always wanted to go and see this festival, but because it was on the last Tuesday of January in Shetland, it just wasn't possible to go and make it back to school for the beginning of the Australian school year, which is also in late January. The day of the festival was blustery, freezing and sleety. I asked my Shetland Da, 'Do they ever cancel it?' He said that the only time it had ever been cancelled was during the First and Second World Wars. It was an exhilarating spectacle. The townspeople gather in the town square in the morning, and the proclamation is read out. Then the Jarl Squad, led by the Guiser Jarl, leads the procession through the town, visiting schools, hospitals and finally being received at the town hall for a ceremony and given the keys to the town. Other squads also take part dressed in costumes depicting the characters they would play in the evening's performance.

The celebration continues all night in all the halls around Lerwick. The Jarl Squad visits each hall and sings a song to much cheering and yelling. Then each of the other groups performs an item they have rehearsed around a theme. That night there were clowns, drag queens, prostitutes, nuns, sexy dancers, and a whole group of

Marylin Monroe look-alikes; it was quite incredible. I had assisted with the preparation for this by putting the makeup on Brenda and Gordon's son, Ben, who was dressed as a buxom milkmaid. This was accompanied by much whisky drinking and merrymaking. I paced myself that night, and I had decided to just drink cider because I wanted to see it all, having waited so long and travelled so far. My kids had said, 'You will probably be under a table by ten o'clock, Mum!' I proved them wrong. I stayed at the celebration, dancing to the fiddle and accordion band that played Scottish jigs and reels all night. The party continued without missing a beat, way into the wee, small hours of the next day. I did a stint in the kitchen with Brenda, serving 'reestit mutton and tattie soup' (a Shetland specialty) with bannocks (Scottish bread) to keep the merrymakers well fed and in high spirits.

It was strange seeing the sky get lighter in the windows of the school hall as the winter sun rose feebly overhead. My cousins told me that the kids of Lerwick have a terrific time the day after Up Helly Aa going on scavenger hunts and finding bits of all the costumes that have been discarded or lost 'aroond da toon'.

I had decided to rent a 'wee hoose' in Lerwick for a couple of months. I didn't want to impose on the rellies for that length of time, and I wanted to really see what it was like living in Shetland. I had rented the house from Bryan, who had been in the Jarl Squad in full Viking splendour. Someone had taken a pic of us very late that night. Bryan worked on an oil rig in the North Sea for weeks at a time and rented out his central Lerwick house. I had met him in my second cousin Anna's pub, The Queen's Hotel, the week before to pay a month's rent in advance and collect the keys.

My Shetland Mam and Da took me to my new place in Lerwick two days after Up Helly Aa. Bryan's family had come from near and far to stay in the house over the week of the festival. They were leaving the day after Up Helly Aa. I was rapt to see that they had left me lots of food in the fridge that they didn't eat and a note saying, 'Help yourself'. The Shetland people are the most generous and kind people that I have ever met. Many people would call my grandparents 'the salt of the earth' when they spoke of them.

Catherine and Rob helped me carry in all my gear, gave me a big hug and left. I started unpacking. I dragged my big pink case upstairs and found the main bedroom. I looked at the bed, and it seemed a bit 'lumpy'. Being the neat freak I am, I started smoothing down the cover. The next thing I knew, a naked man leapt out from under the covers and said, 'Who are you?' I scrambled back down the stairs in fright, and he put on his pants and followed me downstairs shortly afterwards.

It was my landlord Bryan, apologising profusely, saying, 'I am so sorry, we have been partying since the festival ended, and I staggered back here and fell asleep.' Then he said, 'Shit, where is my Viking suit?' He ran back upstairs to check, no Viking suit.

I stood there bewildered, and there was a knock at the front door. I opened the door, and a middle-aged lady said, 'I am the Viking's grandmother and I have just come to see if he has found his Viking suit?' By this stage, I was thinking that maybe Brenda and Gordon were playing a trick on me, and there was a hidden camera. No hidden camera; it was just life in Shetland after a huge week celebrating the Fire Festival. He also had no recollection of us having a photo taken together until I showed him the pic on my phone. The Viking gear costs about two thousand pounds as everything is made totally authentically, right down to the metal fastenings and intricate carvings on the shields. I laughed about this for days and still tell this story quite often.

I spent a lot of time walking around the narrow cobblestone streets of Lerwick; it is so quaint and old. The weather was icy and very blustery. The houses are centrally heated, so you don't realise how cold it is outside. I would look out the window and think, *Yeah*, *looks alright today* and walk outside. I would do an abrupt turn and go back inside the house and 'suit up'. I bought a new coat to wear because my Australian coat was useless, then put on some thick gloves, a scarf and a warm hat. I even bought a pair of earmuffs to wear outside. Catherine and her daughter Susie took me shopping one day, so I could buy more appropriate clothing for Shetland's freezing climate.

I didn't hire a car in Lerwick, and there weren't many people out walking. People would slow down in their cars and look at me strangely as if to say, 'What the hell are you walking around in this weather for?' The Shetland people are so kind and friendly, and I received heaps of lifts home and cups of tea in strangers' houses when I got drenched. I recall standing in the post office in Lerwick one day, totally soaked from head to toe. The lady standing next to me in the line said, 'Och lass, du's soakin, I'll gie dee a run hame.' Which is Shetland for 'You poor bugger, you are soaked; I'll run you home.'

Their 'milk bars' or stores are very different from ours because you can buy wine, beer, and alcohol. So, I was a regular customer at the 'off licence' just around the corner from where I was living. By the end of my stay, they knew me quite well, and we had lots of good chats. I was quite lonely a lot of the time, and Mum sent me postcards of home, which made me homesick. One blizzard-like Saturday, I was really feeling miserable and remembered Jim saying to me, 'You can't run away from yourself, Mum.' I named that particular day 'homesick Saturday' and just sat in front of my fake fireplace drinking and watching TV.

I organised a night out with my cousins in mid-February. We started at my house and had a couple of vinos. We all went to dinner at a Chinese restaurant in Lerwick. I always called it 'The Red Lantern' because there were a lot of red lanterns hanging from the ceiling. The restaurant is really called The Wall, and my cousins always correct me when I refer to it as 'The Red Lantern'. Then we did a pub crawl around the drinking establishments and ended up at The Queen's Hotel. I had visited Anna's lovely establishment several times and was very surprised one day to find that the bartender was from the Gold Coast in Queensland. Nick and I had lots of great chats, and I wanted my cousins to meet him. We ended up at The Marlex, which is also owned by Anna and her husband George. I lost my coat, and the keys to my house were in the pocket. I was quite worse for wear, and I stayed overnight with lovely Brenda, and she took me back to the pub the next morning, and my coat was still there in the corner. Nothing was missing from my coat, not even the twenty pounds I had stuffed into the side pocket. I had a screaming hangover and decided that I would never drink whisky again, and I haven't either!

I stayed in Shetland for nearly eight weeks. I applied for several teaching positions, but I didn't even get one interview. One evening I was checking my Facebook page, and I gasped in shock! A friend had posted a tribute to Sally. I was in disbelief and messaged my friend in Australia. She told me that Sally had taken her own life. I was very distressed and rang Brenda, who dropped everything and came over straight away. She was so kind and supportive and hugged me as I drank myself into oblivion and cried my eyes out.

I was contacted by the lass who had been asked to do Sally's eulogy in my absence. I sat down at my laptop and wrote about our friendship over thirty years and poured out my heart. Jane and Mum went to Sally's funeral and said that she read it out word for word and there wasn't a dry eye in the room.

I wanted to do my own tribute to Sally, and I hired a car. I bought a bunch of white roses and drove to the site of the first house my Poppa had built, called 'The Sparl'. I walked down to the burn in front of the house and said a few words, and sang 'Your Song' by Elton John. I threw the roses one by one into the water, and while I doing that, I felt a great sense of peace came over me. I knew that Sally was finally at rest after being in such turmoil for most of her life. Jane said that everything had been purple at Sally's funeral. Walking back up the muddy bank, I looked down, and there was a purple shell sticking out of the mud. I picked it up and put it in my pocket. When I got back to Australia, Jane gave me the twenty-first birthday picture taken of Sandy, Sally, and me at the party I had thrown that day so long ago. Sally had framed the photo in an intricate, antique frame, and she always kept it beside her bed. I put the shell inside the wire lacework, and it now has pride of place on my bedside table. It is the last thing I see every night before I turn out my lamp.

I went to stay with Brenda and Gordon for several days to attend another Fire Festival celebration that Brenda was helping to organise. I was watching a show on the telly with them; it was the Aussie version of *Come Dine with Me*. I loved the show and watched it every morning while I was there. The accents of the contestants were so 'Strine'. I said to Brenda, 'God, they are bunging it on; there is no way I sound like that.' Brenda was laughing her head off and replied, 'You sound exactly like that, Margy.' I had been away from home for too long! We were cooking tea in Brenda's kitchen that afternoon, and she pulled out a book and gave it to me. 'Do you remember this?' she asked me. I looked at it, and it was the journal with all the recipes that I had given her twenty-five years ago. She said, 'I hope you are going to make your 'World-Famous Lasagne' because my kids have grown up eating it.'

Ben was there and said to me, 'Wow, I can't believe that I am going to really eat Margy's lasagne.' I felt like a celebrity chef, and I made my 'world-famous lasagne' pretending to be Nigella Lawson filming an episode for her TV show, *At My Table*. We laughed ourselves silly and hammed it up for the pretend cameras.

On a trip into Lerwick with Brenda and Gordon, I noticed that there were lots of fishing nets along the street. I casually mentioned to Brenda, 'There must be a lot of fishermen who live in this street, Brenda?' She looked really amused and asked me to repeat the question so Gordon could hear me over the radio in the driver's seat. I repeated the question louder and I noticed that both of them were now laughing out loud in the front seat.

I said, 'What is the bloody joke?'

They could hardly breathe by this stage. I started to think that they had gone mad.

Brenda croaked, 'Do you think that the nets are all for fishing?'

I replied, 'For God's sake, Brenda, why else would there be fishing nets all over the footpath?'

Brenda stopped cackling long enough to explain that the nets were used to put over the rubbish bins to stop them from being blown away in Shetland's fierce winds. I saw the hilarity in the situation and started laughing as well.

I was missing Jim and Ruby terribly, and one day, when I was out walking, I could imagine them as small children running and jumping along beside me. I had always wanted to take them to Scotland to see where their ancestors had come from. It wasn't to be, unfortunately, but life ain't over yet! Well, not until the fat lady sings, and I am determined not to be the fat lady!

I decided that I would return to Australia and went about visiting the rellies and saying goodbye. Catherine and Brenda saw me off at Sumburgh Airport in March 2014, and there is a picture of me howling as I am waving goodbye through the glass partition before I left. I returned to mainland Scotland and spent time with my cousins in Kirkcaldy and Bridge of Earn. I caught a bus back down to England and stayed with my cousin Heather in Cannock for several days.

We had a big night out pretending to be 'Maggie and Heather McSporran 'fae Inverness'. I asked her, 'Can you do a good Scottish accent?'

She replied, 'Och aye, Maggie, ye daft lassie, aye I do a braw Scottish accent.'

So off we went to the local pub and had a very funny night. We stayed in our Scottish personas all night. We told them that we were down visiting our English relatives, and our story got stranger and stranger as the night went on.

The Poms thought we were hilarious, and they shouted us a *lot* of drinks. I was a bit worse for wear at the end of the evening and weaved up to the bartender and said, 'G'day mate, do ya reckon you could call us a cab?'

The guy looked at me strangely and said, 'Blimey, that is the best impersonation of an Aussie accent I have ever heard.'

God, I nearly pissed myself laughing because I had been talking to him earlier in the evening in my Scottish accent, and he thought that I was actually Scottish, not an Aussie.

I spent my last couple of nights in the UK back in London. I stayed just around the corner from Earls Court Station, where we had stayed back in 1988. I wondered again what I would've thought if I had had a time machine and could see into the future back then? I roamed around the city singing 'I'm in London Still' by The Waifs and revisiting my favourite spots. It was early April by then and a tad warmer than when I had last visited in January.

On the long flight back to Melbourne, I reflected on my trip and decided that I was in a much better headspace than I had been when I left. I kept checking the flight map to see where we were, and the thought of hugging my two precious children once more got me through the long, tedious flight. Walking out of the customs gate and seeing Jim, Ruby and Will, was fantastic. I had been all around the world to realise that I had left my heart behind in Australia.

Chapter 15
Burn out

I returned home and lived with Mum and Dad for a couple of weeks. I saw a house advertised for lease in West Warrnambool, and I went around with Mum for a look. I liked it, as it was quite quirky, on a corner block, and the house seemed to follow the block around the corner. The interior was very nineteen eighties with terracotta-coloured laminate benches in the kitchen, daggy old lace curtains on the windows and a bathroom that had a wooden cottage-inspired basin stand. I would've adored this place about the time Bill and I bought our first home, but it had a good 'vibe', and I could see myself living there. I felt much more positive about living alone than I had before I went away. I went to visit my solicitor, who asked me if I had commenced divorce proceedings yet. I said that I wasn't going to worry about it because, like Tom had said, back in 2003, 'I never intend to get married again.' He advised me against this, because in law, you have seven years where you can still claim a share of your former spouse's assets if you don't divorce. He was concerned about my superannuation and encouraged me to start proceedings. I did this, and true to form, Keith made it as difficult as possible.

Ruby was coming up to her twenty-first birthday in September 2014, and I asked her if she would like to go on a holiday to Byron Bay as her gift. Jane and Allan and their families had been holidaying up there for years, and we had never been. Ruby was keen, so I organised flights and accommodation. Divorce number two came through the day before we left on our holiday.

Jim was going to surprise Ruby by turning up to spend the week with us too. I was still quite poor and had only managed to afford a little caravan on a weird block in the industrial part of town. There was a bus and a van that the couple who owned the place rented out. They were into 'world music', and all sorts of strange sounds came from their shed at various times of the day and night. It was great to spend time with the two biggest loves of my life, my kids—and, best of all, we were free from the ogre forever!

I enjoyed my week away with my children and returned to school refreshed. I was working once more with the teacher who had very different ideas and educational objectives to me. She was extremely practical and liked to tick all the boxes, whereas I liked to take a more creative approach to teaching and learning. I soldiered on, trying to keep the peace and go with the flow. It was strange coming back to my old life after spending time alone on the other side of the world. It really made me understand what a huge upheaval my grandparents and Mum and Dad had made in leaving behind everything they had known and worked for to move to a place as far away as they could go. I was still drinking to self-medicate, but I wasn't as sad as I had been before my trip overseas.

I decided to buy a new car. I drove to Melbourne and traded my smoke-blowing Suzuki Grand Vitara in for the minimum five grand trade-in and drove out in my new Mitsubishi Mirage. The first brand new car I had ever driven out of a showroom. I recall driving very cautiously across the West Gate Bridge to Ruby and Will's place in Newport to show them my new car before I drove home to Warrnambool.

A friend of mine was running Zumba classes, and Jane and I decided that we would go. I really needed to get fitter and lose some weight after my travels as I was about ninety kilos and feeling enormous. We became regulars at the class every Saturday morning. This was followed by a coffee catch-up with Mum, Jane, and my

Aunty Grace. This outing quickly became my favourite time of the week because I was moving to music and working up a sweat and then catching up with my family for a chat. We nicknamed ourselves 'The Old Ducks'. When you live alone, you need to have things to look forward to, and this really helped me to stay positive and not drink to excess on Friday nights. I would come home around midday on Saturday and potter around my quirky house doing odd jobs with my bottomless wine glass in hand. I was lonely, but I felt more content and comfortable in my own skin.

In 2015, I decided that it was time to start dating again, and I joined an online dating site. I had messages from a couple of men. I was quite wary about who I would date this time, and I stipulated that I would only consider a non-smoker and non-drinker. I met a couple of guys, and they were quite pleasant, and we had a nice time. It is quite strange meeting someone for the first time when you know that the reason you are there is to interview each other as a possible partner. It is awkward and nerve-racking.

One guy was okay, and we saw each other several times. On a visit to his house after several dates, I was totally freaked out when every inch of his walls had cabinets housing model racing cars. He was also a hoarder. I had dinner, thanked him, and went home.

The next guy was a single dad and cried talking about his kids, which was quite endearing until it continued well into date two.

Man three was a footy fanatic and wore his Collingwood scarf like a badge of honour. I was getting very disillusioned by this stage. I was just about to pull the pin when a guy sent me a lovely message asking me out for dinner. I accepted, and we went for a meal.

Adam was a divorced man with three grown-up children in their twenties. He was easy to talk to, and we got along well. He had a good sense of humour and seemed kind and gentle. He had a self-deprecating manner, and when he smiled, his eyes lit up. I liked him straight away, and after our first date, we both agreed to see one another again. Chemistry is a strange thing: you either have it, or you don't! We had a lot of chemistry, and our relationship progressed quickly. I was happy and enjoying the time we were spending together. It was so lovely to have someone to talk to after school and to share nights, snuggled up on the couch, watching movies with.

Early in our relationship, we went for a weekend down to Lorne on the Great Ocean Road, which is one of my most favourite places in the world. We went to an op shop, and I bought him a hammer, which was funny because he was a plumber. We had lots of laughs visiting art galleries and cafes and staying at the Lorne Cumberland. At breakfast on the last morning, he looked across at me and said, 'I could get very used to this.' My heart was singing. Forever the optimist and an incurable romantic, I started thinking that maybe this time I had found my guy.

The phone rang one evening at my quirky house, and it was Fred's mum Pat, from our first band. We had stayed friends for all these years, and I even saw her for coffee every now and again. She was turning eighty, and she wanted me to sing at her birthday party. I explained that I hadn't sung in public for many years and wasn't very keen to do it. She persisted, and I thought, *Okay, I will get some Linda Ronstadt backing tracks and start rehearsing*. It was great to sing and rehearse once more, and my voice was still there. I learnt my songs inside out, and on the night of the party I thought that I would have a couple of quick drinks to quell the nerves but then remembered that I had never drunk alcohol when I was performing in the past. So, I went to the party sober with Adam, got up on stage and sang my songs. It felt wonderful singing in front of an audience again. I remembered the rush of knowing you were doing a good job, watching the crowd and their reactions and then the applause at the end—the performer's drug.

This performance led to an old bandmate of mine calling me to see if I would be interested in joining his new band. I said, 'Great, when do we start rehearsing?' I loved going to band practice again and, most importantly, having an equal say in the songs we were learning. Another female singer joined the band, and our harmonies were spot on. We developed a great rapport, and she was also a music teacher. This experience was just the tonic I needed to feel like me again. I looked forward to each rehearsal, and like younger me, I learnt my songs inside out. I took great pleasure in being part of a band again.

We had our first gig at a Sunday arvo session at the Warrnambool Hotel, a popular venue in town, and I was nervously excited about performing again after twenty years. Jim, Ruby and their wonderful partners were there to support me. Adam was very supportive and excited for me too. Adam's sister Anne and her friend from Melbourne even turned up to see me perform. The band was very well received, and there was a good crowd. It felt fantastic to sing in public after so long. At the end of the gig, my kids hugged me and told me how proud they were. I felt almost euphoric and just sat by myself after everyone had left the pub and had a couple of drinks. I was on a high and felt like I had found a missing part of myself.

Although my personal life had improved greatly, I was losing enthusiasm for teaching and feeling very anxious before going to school. I was team-teaching with another teacher that I respected greatly. We had known one another for years and had been good friends before I had stuffed it up through my drinking. This class was very challenging with one student who had severe behavioural issues, several students requiring individual learning programs, and an indigenous student who hated coming to school.

We worked hard with this group, and I know that I did my best to deliver a consistent, explicit, and motivating curriculum. I was starting to feel very worn out, and it was an effort to summon the required enthusiasm I once had for the more challenging students. I was also in a new relationship and in the heady new days of being 'loved up'. I stayed at my quirky house on the days I taught and went out to stay with Adam at his place out of town on the weekends and my days off.

Adam had built a unique and spectacular mud-brick house near Koroit. It had an enormous, leadlight feature window which Adam had made himself, and it gave the house quite an 'ecclesiastical' appearance. Adam said that when he had been building the house in the early nineteen eighties, people thought that he was building a church. The first time I was invited to go out to have a meal there, I had to recheck the address Adam had given me to ensure I was in the right place. I had admired this house many years ago when we used to play at the Woolsthorpe Pub not far away. I would say, 'Bill, slow down, that gorgeous house is coming up on the left.' I got out of my car the first time I visited Adam and nearly sank to my knees thinking, *Thank you, Nanna; finally a great guy, and he has a stunning house.*

Adam had two lovely dogs, and we became firm friends very quickly. I spent ages helping him around the place, as it was a bit untidy and needed some TLC to restore it to its former glory. I think that he had let the place go after his wife left him, and the yard was a mess with lots of rubbish strewn around and piles of old junk. So, I was back to running two houses and travelling backwards and forwards. Adam knew that I enjoyed drinking wine, and he quizzed me about it. I told him the truth: that I drank to 'blur' the edges after a fairly traumatic past. Adam wasn't a big drinker himself because it gave him severe headaches, and this was fine with me. I didn't need any encouragement to drink, and it was good because he usually drove when we went out.

One Saturday evening, we had been invited to his sister Anne's place for dinner. She lived just down the road in another lovely house. I had met all his family by then, and I felt that they were supportive of our new relationship. I had opened a bottle of wine and had a couple of glasses before we left. At her place, a bottle of bubbly was popped and we had a couple more. By the time we sat down for dinner, I had consumed quite a bit of wine on an empty stomach, and I was feeling a bit tipsy. In all honesty, I always felt quite nervous around Anne, and she made me feel inferior.

We ate dinner and had more wine, and by then, I was pissed. Adam tapped me abruptly on the shoulder and walked me out to the car, and we went home. I staggered up the stairs to bed, and when I woke up I had that *Oh no, what happened?* feeling again. Adam was furious that I had got drunk at his sister's place and went out for a ride on his motorbike. Anne and her friends from Melbourne came down mid-morning with my coat that I had left behind at her place, and I was mortified.

Adam was unimpressed and told me that I was an alcoholic and that I needed to go to counselling. I was fairly stunned by this, as I had never thought of myself as an 'alcoholic', and I thought he was overreacting. He sent me a text just before class one morning, saying that he was having second thoughts about our relationship and that it might be best to end it. I was very upset about this and replied, *Please come around to my place so we can discuss this.* He had also confided in his previous partner, and she had told me that he wanted to break it off. We discussed this at my place, and I agreed to attend an Alcoholics Anonymous meeting.

This was a whole new ball game, and I was very nervous walking in for the first time. The people at AA were lovely and supportive, and I felt much better after my initial visit. Alcohol doesn't discriminate, and there were ladies my age, young people in their twenties and thirties and several members who had been attending for years. Their stories were very raw and emotional; many people had hit rock bottom and lost everything because of alcohol. I knew that I had never gone that far into total self-destruction and that I was lucky that I had a supportive family.

I continued going to AA meetings weekly, and I cut down my drinking a lot. I was very stressed at school, though, and still drank quite a lot to chill out at the end of a stressful day. This was the first time that I became aware that I had a real dependence on alcohol. I started feeling awkward about drinking around anyone, and so I just drank by myself at home. I wasn't wiping myself out but drinking enough to take the edge off things and help me relax. I used to take my recycling bin out under cover of darkness because the wine bottles inside it rattled and clinked so much. When Adam was at my place I hid my glass, or I would pretend that I was drinking a cup of tea when it was wine. I began drinking secretly around him because I knew he didn't like it.

Adam had been in a serious motorbike accident about ten years earlier. He had nearly lost his life and had been in hospital for months recuperating. Physically, he had recovered very well and was even back working full-time. He did have an acquired brain injury and suffered from severe headaches at times. He also became tired very quickly and spent a lot of time either asleep on the couch or in bed. I was fine with this and would just amuse myself by playing my online games or checking out Facebook.

I was a tad concerned about the story he gave me that his ex-wife had just left one evening without any warning. That just isn't how life works. Having been divorced twice, you know when your relationship is not working and, *hopefully,* you see the signs and address them. A friend of Adam's told me, 'There was no love left in that house.' He had very little social awareness. He said silly things a lot, and he also couldn't empathise when I explained how I was feeling about something.

He would pretend to be crying if something happened that he didn't like, which to me seemed weak and pathetic. A classic example of this was when I told him about the awful trip to Sydney with my ex-friend Toni and the total verbal castigation that she had given me. Adam said, 'Fair enough, I *kinda* see where she is coming from.'

Huh? I explained that even if he thought she had been correct in her observations, you *always* take your partner's corner. He just didn't pick up on social cues and could be extremely difficult to communicate with. Once again, the red flags were flying, but I had turned a blind eye to the things I didn't like, thinking that no-one was perfect.

My lease on the quirky house was coming up for renewal in April 2016, and Adam suggested, 'Why don't you move in with me?' I thought about it carefully, and I didn't rush my response. I was worried that if I lived with him, there would be no way to hide how much I drank. I decided to go ahead and move in as I was very tired of cleaning two houses, weeding two gardens, and paying a lot of money for a place I hardly lived in. My neatness had followed me from my teenage years, and my kids even call me the 'neat freak'.

The real estate agents I had dealt with regarding my quirky house were terrible. I take great pride in the places I live in, even when they don't belong to me. I had sanded and stained the wooden vanity unit in the bathroom, hung new curtains in the main bedroom, put in a couple of new light fittings and generally kept the house and garden very tidy.

They were refusing to give me back my bond, saying that the front garden was very overgrown. I looked at the pictures of the place from the old adverts I had, and the plants then were small, indicating that these pictures were quite old. I got an arborist to help me prune back the shrubs and trees. They still weren't satisfied. A verbal and written battle ensued, and they were going to take me to VCAT. I cried when that letter came in the mail. I went down to their office to ask why they were doing this to me when I had been a reliable and clean tenant? They admitted they had made a mistake. I received my full bond money back and made a mental note never to deal with them again.

I moved out to Adam's place on April Fool's Day 2016: how prophetic! He had been trimming back trees on his property at the time, and there were branches everywhere. It was chaotic trying to move my furniture in while branches were lying all over the grounds. I did say to Adam, 'I don't do mess.' He could get very overwhelmed by small problems and trivial matters.

I did the bulk of the moving by myself over a couple of weeks, taking the smaller items out by car and putting the bigger furniture items on Adam's work ute. I was excited to be moving into the house and looking forward to setting the place up nicely. He had left that morning to be a helper on his motorbike in the Murray to Moyne bike race.

I thought it would be nice to spend the day placing my clothes in the drawers and ornaments and belongings on the shelves. I was in the kitchen at lunchtime and saw that I had missed a call from him. I was about to ring him back, and my phone rang again. It was Adam saying that he had come around a corner on his bike and lost control. The ambulance was there, about to take him to hospital. I thought he was playing an April fool's joke on me, but he said, 'Talk to the ambo then.' I drove to the hospital and found him in the emergency room with a broken collarbone.

The next three months were not fun. I did all the domestics, carted wood inside for the wood heater, purchased all our groceries, cooked all our meals and looked after my patient. It was a baptism of fire, really, and I was also teaching and rehearsing with the band. His sister, Anne, had said to me, 'Good luck being Adam's nurse; he is a very demanding patient.' The understatement of the year!

One night on my way to band practice, I asked him to turn on the oven at six o'clock. I had made a chicken casserole and thought it would be ready by the time I got home from rehearsal. I arrived home, and the oven wasn't turned on, so no dinner. I was a bit cranky and asked him why he hadn't turned on the oven. He said, 'I have been resting on the couch, and I forgot.' He enjoyed being the helpless invalid and took it to extremes. I am glad that I was a teacher and not a nurse or doctor because I have a very low tolerance for people who whine and moan. In my family, you had to be near death to see a doctor or get medical assistance.

We had a trip to Sydney for a few days during this time, and I was quite astonished by how flustered he became when travelling. I was glad that we were only going to Sydney and not the UK. We stayed at the Shangri La Hotel, which was very flash and had a panoramic view of Sydney Harbour from our suite. On the first night, I decided to have a bath in the marble tub and poured myself a glass of wine. Adam was really cross about this and said, 'We have already had wine with our dinner.' I was quite upfront about having it and was perplexed as to why he was so cross. After the wine-in-the-bath drama, I was quite unsure whether to order any drinks. I found it difficult to censor myself and decided in the end to just order non-alcoholic drinks. I was disappointed, and I felt like he was monitoring me.

The rest of 2016 passed without too many incidents. I was very careful not to upset Adam in any way, even if I didn't agree with what he said. There was a definite pattern emerging there, and I was just repeating the same old scenario over and over. I kept going to AA and listened and joined in at meetings. I did find it quite repetitive to hear the same stories week in and week out. The original 'Big Book' of examples used to illustrate the perils of alcoholism was written in 1939 and is very sexist in its language. I know that AA has helped millions of people to get sober and stay sober, but it just wasn't my thing. I would go to my meeting and then buy wine on my way home. It just hadn't 'clicked' in my brain. I was also very conscious of being recognised when I went to meetings. Warrnambool isn't a huge place, and when I parked my car outside at meetings, I thought it was obvious where I was going, so there was no anonymity for me. I was ashamed and embarrassed, and this wasn't helping me to remain sober.

I had been asked by an acquaintance if I would speak at the Southwest Depression and Anxiety Group meeting in Warrnambool, and I agreed to do this. I found that writing about my journey was very therapeutic. I stood up and spoke for the first time about my struggle with depression and anxiety and my dependence on alcohol, and it felt like a burden had been lifted from my shoulders.

Adam and I joined Jane, and Allan, and their families on the annual trip to Byron Bay that September and stayed in a nice cabin in a caravan park, and we hired a little car. It was an enjoyable trip, and we drove around admiring the sights, visiting hinterland villages like Nimbin—a cartoonish throwback village to the seventies pot culture. At Jane's caravan site one morning, she looked very upset and said that she had received the news that Mum had been diagnosed with cervical cancer. We were quite distraught and tried to work out the best way to deal with the news.

Once home, we agreed that we would accompany Mum to Melbourne for her operation to remove the cancer at the Royal Women's Hospital. Jane, Dad and I accompanied Mum to Melbourne, and we stayed in an apartment near the hospital. It was a scary time, and I don't think anyone is ever prepared for the news that a loved one has a life-threatening illness.

I felt strange walking with my family and Mum to the hospital the morning she was admitted. I tried to imprint the footage of us walking together inside my brain. Mum is a very brave woman and gave no outward sign that she was nervous or scared. Hugging her before she went in for surgery, my heart was banging wildly inside my chest, and I prayed to the powers that be to let me have my beautiful, irreplaceable mum back healthy and whole.

We spent several days in the apartment in Melbourne. It was during the time that Trump was running for president. Dad and I watched his 'debate' with Hilary Clinton on TV one afternoon. I turned to Dad and said, 'There is no way that belligerent, orange, sexist fool will become president of the United States.' Dad agreed with me, and we watched the debate shaking our heads at Trump's overbearing rudeness and sense of bombastic superiority. He reminded me of Bill.

We were overjoyed when Mum was given the news that the operation was a total success. She would have to return to Melbourne for check-ups every six months, but we reckoned that was a bargain compared to the alternative.

Adam and I hosted Christmas at his place that year. He was renovating the outdoor barbeque area, and on Christmas Eve, it still wasn't finished. Like every other year, the lead up to Christmas and the end of the year at school had been hectic and exhausting. I wanted the place to look fantastic because I had told everyone how unique and original the place was, and I was looking forward to their reactions. I had watched all the YouTube clips on how to cook the perfect turkey, and it was stuffed and ready to go on Christmas morning. I could still hear Adam hammering in nails while I was preparing our Christmas lunch, and I was stressed out of my brain.

Ruby arrived early, and she could tell straight away that I was struggling to get on top of things and pitched in to help me. It was about thirty-five degrees as well, and I was hot, tired, cranky and anxious that the food wouldn't be ready on time or that there wasn't enough. Meanwhile, Adam was just sitting with Allan and my brother-in-law, drinking beer. I felt cross, and, as usual, I just buried my anger and tried to get through the day.

Adam had invited his children out for Christmas dinner, and it was too much after doing lunch. I said, 'They will just have to have leftovers because I am not cooking anything else.' He was definitely from the male generation who thought that their main job was to make sure everyone had a drink in their hand and a comfy seat to tell jokes from.

A couple of days later, I said to Adam that he could've helped more on Christmas Day, and it wasn't fair that I had done the bulk of the work. He was sitting outside by himself in the barbeque area.

I was cross with him, and he hated to be challenged or deal with any confrontations at all. Ruby was staying with us, and I had vented to her about it. She is quite an astute young woman and said to me, 'Who are you trying to be at the moment, Mum, because you are not yourself.' You cannot fool your children or your mum if you are not being your true self.

I slept downstairs that night in protest, and the next morning he opened the door of the spare bedroom and said, 'I want you to leave; find another place to live.' I was totally gobsmacked that one argument had led to this. He went to work, and Ruby and I decided just to go to her place in Melbourne for a couple of days to let him have some space. It was New Year's Eve by then, and I just bought wine and drank myself silly. I was terrified that I would have to go through the whole moving-house saga again, be alone again and try to survive again.

I resolved to go back with my cap in hand, eat humble pie and apologise for my outburst, blaming total exhaustion for my crime of speaking up. I drove home with my heart in my throat. I had also been hiding how much I was drinking from Ruby as well, so I stopped at a bin in Winchelsea and got rid of all the empty wine bottles in the boot of my car. I arrived back at Adam's place, and he wasn't home, so I played with the dogs for a while. I decided to write him a letter to explain how I was feeling and tell him that I would try harder to stop drinking and be a less troublesome partner. I read the letter to him when he did arrive home, and we discussed the situation in depth. Adam said that he respected my honesty and that we would continue our relationship provided that I maintained my sobriety and I didn't cause him any *undue stress.*

We started 2017 on a better note. I maintained my role as housekeeper, groundswoman, and boarder in a polite fashion. I resolved to never complain, be amiable and just smile and nod a lot. I had my wine hidden in various hidey-holes around the place and drank a lot. It was a huge job maintaining three acres of grounds and keeping a mud-brick house free from dust and cobwebs. I worked extremely hard to keep the place looking tidy and welcoming. Friends of Adam's had said to me how much better the house and gardens looked now that they were being cared for. My lovely next-door neighbour had said that I had turned the house into a home again.

I was teaching with a new partner who I got along with very well. She was easy to talk to, and we were both on the same page in our teaching pedagogy and style. I could feel myself winding down through my gears, though, and it was becoming harder and harder to get out of bed and drive to school. *Get in the car and go to school now*, the little conscientious part of my brain would shriek. *No, I can't do it; please don't make me go*, the anxious, tired, and worn out part of my brain would reply. I was pushing myself to keep going and getting worried that I wouldn't be able to keep up the effort required to do this for long.

I hired a skip to clean up all the rubbish in front of the shed over Easter. I had to show Adam everything I put in the skip to make sure he didn't want to keep it, right down to old rusty hinges and nails. I had my teeth clenched during this process so I that I wouldn't scream at him. There was everything from old piles of paper and bits of metal to cardboard boxes, old tools, rusty crap, and old plumbing stuff. It was a bloody eyesore, and I couldn't stand looking at it anymore. I paid a guy who helped me from time to time in the garden to help us put the crap in the skip—he didn't have to show Adam what he was throwing away. We filled a large skip with that rubbish, and the place looked less like a tip.

I had totally lost my passion for teaching by now. During the night, I was going downstairs and sitting at the dining room table by myself and worrying about the next day. I was getting up in the morning before school and saying to myself, *Get in the bloody car and go to school.* Another voice in my head was saying, *I just can't do this anymore; I feel sick.*

This persisted until the winter school holidays when I went into school to do some work one day. I came in and sat behind my desk, looked up and thought, *I can't be here anymore.* I got up and went to leave when a voice from the adjoining classroom said, 'Did you leave something in your car, Margy?'

I replied, 'No, I can't do this anymore.'

My colleague came into the room and said, 'What do you mean?'

I told her that I was *done* and I wouldn't be returning to school. The look on her face was priceless!

I had organised to have lunch that day with my lovely old friend, Goldie, from my shared specialist teaching days. Goldie had been my main supporter when I had written and produced *Superheroes,* and we had remained firm friends over the years. I told her the story, and she wasn't surprised, having left teaching herself not long before this. She gave me the name of the guy she had dealt with in the superannuation branch, ESS Super in Melbourne. ESS Super is the superannuation company that the Education Department uses for teachers as well as emergency workers. She told me to call him because he had helped her to navigate early retirement and had been sympathetic and very efficient.

I was going down to Melbourne to see the kids over the school holidays anyway, and I made an appointment with the man Goldie recommended. I wanted to meet with him in person to discuss my options for early retirement. He agreed, so into Williams Street I went for our meeting. The Emergency Services and State Super office at 140 Williams Street, Melbourne, is in a tall glass and chrome building which is very intimidating and flash. I went up to the sixteenth floor and sat in the waiting area.

A tall, grey-haired gentleman appeared and introduced himself, and we went to his office. He asked me to tell him about my career and why I was wanting early retirement. I told him briefly about my teaching roles over the past thirty-two years and my struggles with anxiety, depression, domestic violence, and alcoholism. He was very sympathetic and said to me, 'You wouldn't believe how many people have sat in the chair where you are sitting now and told me a similar story. You are burnt out, and I will help you to retire.' He did all the sums and showed me that I would be able to convert my super to a fortnightly pension.

He suggested that I take the rest of my long service leave and then my sick leave if necessary, to enable me to retire from teaching immediately. I cried with relief, and then I cried even harder because someone was taking the time to listen to me with such kindness and concern. It was like a concrete block being lifted off my shoulders. I stood outside the office block on the pavement for ages bawling like a baby.

There were businesspeople rushing by with their briefcases, barking into their phones and looking at me as if I was a lunatic. I was sobbing my heart out, and I didn't care. All I knew is that I would never have to make myself get into my car with my stomach in knots, wanting to be sick and go to a job that I had found extremely stressful and difficult for thirty-two years.

Chapter 16
Retirement

In my first three months of retirement, I slept. I was bone tired and would often wake up at ten o'clock in the morning after sleeping for twelve hours. I guess my mind and body needed to recover from the years of stress and anxiety. I walked the dogs a lot and I just allowed myself to rest.

I was given a retirement morning tea at school, and a lovely colleague, Gina, had even made me a cake shaped like a guitar. I really hadn't wanted any fuss at all. I just wanted to go quietly. I also had the feeling that quite a few of my colleagues were upset that I had gone out on a 'disability'. This was upsetting to me because I'd never told anyone at school about my anxiety and depression or my alcohol dependence. I think several of my colleagues knew about the domestic violence I had suffered, but it wasn't common knowledge.

I had to go to Melbourne to be assessed by two consultant psychiatrists in order to qualify for my disability pension. I was quite nervous about attending these appointments, but Jim and Ruby said in jest, 'Just act a little bit crazier than you usually do, and you will get it.' I saw both these specialists on the same day in Melbourne. The sessions were both quite lengthy and very thorough, examining my mental health history and substance abuse. While I was in town, I treated myself to a makeover and did some retail therapy. Jim and Ruby took me out for dinner, and I thought I resembled a drag queen with all the makeup I was wearing.

I was very overweight and unfit. I weighed ninety-three kilos by this time and decided to improve my physical fitness. I was twice the person in size that I had been back in 1983 when I had married Bill. I went back to Melbourne in August and did my Zumba instructor training. I was still attending Zumba classes, and I loved it. I rehearsed my moves at home until I had them down pat and decided to start running my own classes.

I set a goal to lose thirty kilograms. I was still drinking, though, so I was sabotaging my own efforts most of the time. I worked like a demon to get fit and would often accrue 20,000 steps on my Fitbit watch daily. I commenced my own Zumba classes in mid-2018 and hired country halls to hold them in. The classes attracted a small, loyal following, but I didn't really care because I was getting fitter and healthier too.

Adam and I took a trip to Tassie in September, travelling around in his Toyota 'Troopy' van, camping and staying in some hotels and cabins. One night in a cabin in Strahan, I checked my emails and was rapt to see one from ESS Super, letting me know that my retirement on disability grounds had been approved. I would receive a pension for life. I jumped up and down with excitement and toasted my new freedom. While we were staying in Hobart, I caught up with the drummer from my first band. His new band were playing in a pub in the city, and he invited me to get up and do a few songs with them. It was great fun, and the crowd were very receptive.

I took some of my super as a lump sum and decided to buy a fancier car. I had been very keen on the Hyundai Veloster because of its sporty appearance. I looked at several, but then I checked out an online auction and saw a lovely bronze Mercedes Elegance coupe for sale in Melbourne. I decided to bid on it and sat with my fingers crossed, watching the bids online until the auction was over. I won!

I cried when I saw my Merc for the first time. Never in a million years did I think I would ever own such a gorgeous car. I told the salesman that I had been keen on buying a Veloster before I saw the Mercedes. He replied, 'Why would you buy a toaster when you can have the whole kitchen?' I was quite tentative driving it home and prayed that someone wouldn't wake me up from the incredible dream I seemed to be having. I gave my little Mirage, fondly named 'Mitsi', to Jim and Lisa because I could and helped the kids out with some money each. Then I decided that we needed to put aircon in the house because it was boiling in the summer. I had spent a lot of money already improving the house, but I figured it was my home too, and I liked to contribute. The aircon went in before Christmas, and it was lovely being cool in the house.

I was still very cautious around Adam. I was absolutely terrified of being asked to leave, and I hid my drinking well. It is a very frightening way to live when you are worried about being evicted at any time. He spent a lot of time on the couch or in bed anyway, so it wasn't that hard to drink in secret. In front of him or in the company, though, I never drank alcohol, and this double life was very stressful and hard to maintain. A couple of times, he found my hiding place and threw the cask at me or filled up my glass beside my bed with vodka or gin. It wasn't good at all, and our relationship became platonic.

He had a very strained relationship with two of his three children, and the rare times they did come to visit were filled with awkward silences, which I tried to fill with silly chatter. One Saturday morning, they were coming for breakfast, which I found a bit odd. My family usually caught up for brunch or lunch, not breakfast. I decided to have a good tidy up and not go to Zumba, thinking that it would be rude not to be present when they were there. Anne arrived first and said, looking down her nose at me, 'I thought you did something *else* on Saturday mornings; this is just for the family, you know.' Ouch! Anne had pointed out very clearly that I wasn't family and, therefore, I wasn't welcome. I ran to the bathroom crying, got my towel, water bottle, and car keys and headed off to my Zumba class.

I had made a big difference in my fitness, and my resting heart rate had gone from 93 beats per minute to 63 beats per minute. I had lost about fifteen kilos at that stage, and I was feeling fitter. My classes were being well attended, and I was proud of myself for achieving this without much support from anyone. I realised that my family were all very busy working, but I did feel peeved that no-one had come to one class to support me, even just to sit at the door and collect the money.

Dad had started to fail a bit. He had always prided himself on being a very fit man, having walked daily and ridden his bike well into his eighties. We all started going to doctors' appointments with him to ask his doctor any questions relating to his prostate cancer. It had been diagnosed over twenty years ago, and they had decided not to remove it surgically because it is very common in older men. It had started to become more aggressive as Dad aged, and he was having injections in his stomach to slow it down. Mum looked after Dad with total selflessness and love so that he could remain at home, and we all pitched in and helped her.

New Year 2018 saw us camping for a couple of weeks in Bridgeport, South Australia. We had been before and really liked the atmosphere, and the caravan park was situated right beside the beach. The dogs liked it too and came with us on holidays. I managed to hide my vodka bottle in my backpack and go to buy refills when Adam was napping. He wasn't the most fun person to holiday with and marched to his own drum and agenda. I did my own thing, too, and even wrote a long letter to Jimmy Barnes in the van after reading his two books. I felt that we had a lot in common having a Scottish background, playing music, and struggling with substance abuse. I even told him that I had seen Cold Chisel play back in the late seventies at the Lady Bay Hotel in Warrnambool when he had been swigging from a bottle of vodka, standing on a table and kicking people's jugs of beer over. I managed to contact a journalist that had interviewed Jimmy recently for the local newspaper where he lives in rural NSW. I asked her if she would forward the letter to him if I sent it to her. She was very helpful, and she agreed to do this for me. I posted the letter, but I never received a reply. If you are reading this book, Jimmy, I hope you got my letter. Cheers!

I continued to be the head chef and groundsperson who didn't complain much. I lived in fear of upsetting Adam, and it was becoming harder to disregard my own feelings and needs. He had some whacky ideas about taking health supplements and various homemade concoctions after watching a self-proclaimed cancer-curing guru—on YouTube. He attempted to get me to take these life-saving remedies, which smelt and tasted like chlorine pool water, but my counsellor told me that I had enough on my plate with trying to abstain from alcohol without taking this on board as well.

I had seen a side of Adam a couple of times that was a bit scary. He asked me one afternoon where his rake was when I was in his shed tidying up. I said that it was down the back with all the other gardening tools. He flew up and grabbed me by the throat and held me against the shed wall, and snarled, 'Stop putting my things away in different places.' I was shocked, and I went back inside shaking. I had flashbacks to my years with Keith and the pain that he had inflicted on me. He was terribly apologetic about his behaviour, and after a while, I thought I had just imagined it.

Life went on, and it was my birthday. I have always made a big fuss of people's birthdays and I like to surprise them with wonderful, thoughtful gifts. For Adam's birthday the first year we were together, I had driven up to Melbourne and back in one day to pick up an antique globe of the world on a stand. He had admired it when we had spent a weekend in the city.

On the morning of my birthday, there was a present on my placemat at the dining room table. Adam had gone to work, but a note said to open it. I slowly opened my present in excited anticipation. It was a tub of Lightning Jell, industrial strength hand cleaner. I cautiously opened the lid and peeked inside the tub to see if there was something there; no, there was just hand cleaner. I was disappointed; NO, I was *bloody* upset and thought about all the lovely gifts I had given him. I didn't think it was funny or slightly amusing. I rewrapped it feeling very hardly done by and put it on his side of the table with the note, 'This is not an acceptable gift. Try again.'

This didn't go down well at all, and he really couldn't understand why I was upset. We discussed it, and I told him that I was living in fear of being evicted at any moment and that it was a huge stress for me. Then I got the most unromantic proposal of all time when he said, 'Would you feel more secure if we got engaged?' I replied that it would make me feel less like a boarder and so we got engaged. No-one was happy for us, and his children didn't even mention it. Anne said, 'That is the most ridiculous thing I have ever heard,' to which I had absolutely no idea how to respond.

I asked if I was going to receive an engagement ring, and he was fairly non-committal. I went by myself to the jewellery store and bought a ring. I just wanted to have a home and security so much that I was prepared to pay any price for it. He didn't even pay for the ring. I bought my own engagement ring. I don't know why I thought this was okay because it absolutely was not. I had also booked and paid for the registry office in Melbourne for a May 2019 wedding, an afternoon tea at the Windsor Hotel across the road, and a ten-day 'honeymoon' at the Village Resort in Phuket, Thailand.

An old colleague, Joy, from my early teaching years came to visit us in the July school holidays. We had stayed in touch by letter and phone over the years, and it was wonderful to see her again. She knew a lot about my bumpy journey and had always been a sympathetic friend and listened to my troubles or gave me her advice when I asked her for it. She quizzed me a fair bit about our relationship, and

I said that it was okay. I don't think she was convinced that we made a good couple. I also showed her my hiding spots for my grog, and she said that she was worried about this. Adam had come in while I was in the middle of showing her, and once again, I was sprung. He stomped upstairs, and I tried to talk to him, but he wouldn't listen. Joy sat with him and explained that I needed his support and help, not constant accusations and telling off.

After this, I went to the drug and alcohol rehabilitation centre and had an assessment done. I went to the Western Region Alcohol and Drug Centre (WRAD) and received weekly counselling and monitoring. Each Tuesday afternoon, I visited the Warrnambool Base Hospital for a session with the drug and alcohol nurse. I also joined the UK-based online group, 'Club Soda Alcohol-Free', which is a fantastic group committed to helping people trying to give up drinking. I met lots of like-minded souls who provided me with support and advice about abstaining from alcohol. We all liked to swap stories about our dysfunctional relationship with 'the wine witch' and how to break the habit. I ordered and read the book by Annie Grace called *This Naked Mind*, and it totally changed the way I thought about alcohol. I was doing everything in my power to address my alcohol dependence.

Towards the end of the year, we had a nice dinner out in the barbeque area, and I had a small piccolo of bubby. I poured it into a glass, thinking that it would be nice to have a glass with dinner. Adam came in and took a sip from my glass and said, 'Still at it; I can't trust you at all.' We limped on and one day, having lunch in town, I said, 'It would be nice to take a trip to Scotland together maybe after we get married.'

He replied, 'That's not going to happen; there will be no wedding.'

I was gutted, absolutely unsure about what to do and totally stuffed. I dropped him back at work that day and asked him, 'Are we still engaged, or is that cancelled too?'

He replied, 'We can stay engaged and still go on the trip, but I don't want to marry you.'

I blundered on; that is the only way I can describe it. I was ashamed, broken, and very disillusioned.

I was seeing a psychologist and trying to work through my self-worth issues and just have someone I could talk to. I spoke about the whole engagement fiasco, and she tried to get me to elaborate on why it was so important to me to get married. I think it was a sense of wanting the security and status of having a husband and a home, even if that meant sacrificing my own self-worth once more. She made me think about what would really happen if 'the branch broke' and I was on my own again. I realised that financially I would be okay, but it still terrified me to think of being alone again.

I was also talking about my children, and she said that she had heard Jim's music and that I must be so proud of my kids and what they had achieved. I replied with the usual response I give, 'I don't know how they turned out so well considering I am such a disaster.' She looked incredulous and asked me to repeat what I had said. She looked at me fair and square and said, 'Your children have turned out the way they did because you are a fantastic mum; luck has nothing to do with it.' No-one had ever said that to me before or paid me that enormous compliment, and I felt a tear trickle down my face. I responded by saying that I know that I have made many mistakes, but there wasn't one second of one day where my children didn't know how much they were loved.

Christmas came around, and we had carols at our place. Ruby played the portable keyboard that she borrowed from a friend, and we invited our neighbours and friends in for a night of singing and music. I hadn't touched a drop of alcohol for a couple of weeks after the last episode with the piccolo of bubby. It was so weird not having a champers or Baileys on Christmas Eve. I actually said to Adam, 'I think this is the first Christmas Eve since I was about ten that I haven't had one alcoholic drink.' Even as kids, Nanna had given us a little glass of Stone's Green Ginger Wine on Christmas Eve. He did not understand what a big deal this was for me, and there was no 'Well done' or 'I am proud of you.' It was just expected that I would 'toe the line' or leave.

Adam and I caught up with the extended family on Christmas Day. Jim and Lisa came home for a couple of days, and things were okay. We all went on our annual beach walk from Killarney to Port Fairy on Boxing Day and had lunch together. The kids went home after Boxing Day, and it was just Adam and me at home again.

I had just made some banana bread after doing a Zumba practice class in the lounge room. Adam came in from outside, and I said, 'Let's sit down and have a chat and a cuppa.'

I had a real sense that things were off, so I asked him if everything was okay. He was being very difficult to talk to, so I said, 'Look, this is what you might have done in your former relationship, but I believe in talking things through if there is a problem that we need to address, not bury our heads in the sand.'

With that, he stood up and threw his hot cup of tea at me. I ducked under the table because it was boiling water, and I didn't want to get burnt. Then he started hurling fruit from the fruit bowl: apples, grapes, and an orange. He came up to me and smeared me with an overripe mango all over my head. He was just out of control and going berserk, yelling obscenities at me and screaming *'Get out of my house!'* I was in total shock that this had escalated into a physical attack with absolutely no warning. It had gone from zero to a hundred in a matter of seconds. He stormed out, cursing and terrified, I ran to the bathroom to have a look at myself. I was dripping with fruit. I went back to the kitchen and got my phone from the charger and took a picture of the kitchen floor because I didn't think that anyone would believe me. There was squashed fruit all over the floor, overturned chairs, smashed cups and plates, and it looked like a bar room brawl had just taken place.

I went upstairs, watching fruit drop off me onto the steps, and threw some stuff in a bag. I went to the kitchen and grabbed my car keys. Outside by my car, he was throwing stuff in the boot, ranting and raving and yelling at me, *'Get out you fucking bitch and take your shit with you!'* I drove down to Anne's place because I wanted her to see what he had done. She wasn't home, so I drove back into my mum and dad's place in town. Once I was there, I had no recollection of how I got there. I was in shock and shaking from head to toe. Mum and Dad were away on holidays, so I rang Ruby, and she said, 'I will be straight there.'

Chapter 17
Alone again, naturally

Mum, Dad, Jane and Allan had gone up to Mackay to see my great uncle. I had been invited to go too, but I had decided not to go as the kids were coming home for Christmas. I found the key to their front door and went inside. I was covered in bits of fruit, and my hair was stiff and sticking up like Cameron Diaz's hair in that funny scene in the movie, *There's Something About Mary*. It was quite surreal, and I wasn't sure what had just occurred.

I zipped up to the bottle shop and bought some wine and vodka. The universe was really being spiteful that day because when I selected my wine and stood up in the wine aisle, who should be standing there? My old friend Toni, who had ruined my Opera House experience. I ducked down in panic, hoping that she hadn't seen me looking like a swamp creature. Her prophecy had come true, I had stuffed it up yet again.

I went back to Mum and Dad's and started drinking. Ruby turned up and tried hard to comfort me, but I was a mess. I alternated between lying down and sobbing on Mum's side of the bed and cursing and drinking to block out reality. I rang a friend in England who had been in my online group, Club Soda Alcohol-Free. I wasn't coherent by that stage. I just wanted to die. I had totally given up.

On New Year's Day, I rang Lifeline and spoke to a lovely young man who wanted to know if I was having suicidal thoughts. I told him that I was, and he stayed on the phone talking to me for ages.

He talked me down, and I assured him that I wouldn't harm myself. I was very unwell, and once again, I felt like I was walking through pea soup. My legs and arms felt heavy, and my stomach was sore, and it hurt to breathe.

Ruby is a kind, caring and strong young woman. She stayed with me, made sure I ate some food, put me to bed and told me that it would be okay. I didn't believe that for one second; I thought my life was now over. She took me out for the day and kept an eye on me. Adam messaged me to say that he was going to come around and speak to me. I was extremely nervous and wasn't sure how to react. Ruby stayed with me for support as Adam said his piece.

Sitting at Mum and Dad's dining room table, he said, to our combined astonishment, 'It was lucky I didn't kill you because I would now be in jail, and you would be in the morgue.'

I kid you not! Ruby was very forthright and said to him, 'You owe my mother an apology, Adam. What you did to her was totally inappropriate no matter what you thought she had done to deserve it.'

He looked a bit taken by surprise. Adam wasn't used to someone not agreeing with him and making him accountable for his narcissistic behaviour. He muttered, 'Sorry,' under his breath and continued his spiel.

He said that it was over, he would not be responsible for me anymore, and that I would have to remove my furniture and belongings from his house. He was so smug while he was talking, and it crossed my mind that although my other past partners had treated me very poorly, they had not masqueraded as Mr Nice Guy. Adam was the scariest one of them all because he had totally abused my trust while pretending that he was my knight in shining armour. He continued by saying that he would pay me some money for the improvements I had made to the place, and I was to collect my things as quickly as possible. I was still in zombie mode and didn't say a lot. He left, and I haven't spoken to him in person since.

Mum and Dad came home from their trip. I hadn't told them that I was there because I didn't want them to worry or spoil their holiday. Mum came in and gave me the biggest hug. I didn't have to say anything; she just knew. Dad was really struggling by this time. He spent a lot of time in bed sleeping, which was just not like him. It was strange to see him in bed at eleven in the morning. Mum was selfless as always in looking after him and, as usual, put his needs above her own.

I needed a break, and I went to Lorne for a couple of days. I always feel centred in Lorne, as it is my 'happy place'. I just walked on the beach and sat on the front balcony of the pub, drinking and watching the tourists, birds, and sea. I once again had to work out where I was going to live and what I was going to do. I was so very low. My thoughts were swirling around in my head like the seagulls overhead with the ever-familiar voice saying, 'See, you aren't good enough, you will never be good enough, no-one wants you.'

I went up to Melbourne to help Ruby clean her unit. She had finished her teaching degree and had been successful in obtaining a teaching position, so she was moving back home. I had been looking online for possible rentals but hadn't seen anything I liked so far. I am the type of person that must really like my home and be able to see myself there before I move into it. Ruby put a real estate app on my phone, and I was having a look when I saw a place I really liked. I rang the agent who said, 'I just put it up online about ten minutes ago.' I asked when I could have a look at it, and she said, 'Today.' I got in the Merc, drove down the Princes Highway and went to inspect the place. I loved it and hoped and prayed that I would be the successful applicant. Thankfully, the agent rang me the next day to tell me that I could move in the following week.

I hired a removalist to collect my furniture from Adam's house, and Ruby and I moved the smaller items in our cars. Adam's eldest son had been given the job of supervising my departure and just sat and watched as Ruby and I took load after load to our cars. It felt very strange to be taking all my things out of the house after having such high hopes that I had finally found a nice partner and home. Adam's house looked very bare after I removed my furniture and possessions.

I started to feel a bit better being in my new home. Ruby was going to stay with me for term one because the place she and Will were moving into wasn't available yet. I was so happy to have my girl at home with me, and we enjoyed watching our girly shows on Netflix. I found her company soothing.

Dad had decided that he would start chemotherapy for his prostate cancer. His first treatment was on the day of the Academy Awards in Hollywood. I have loved watching the Academy Awards since I was a child and never miss it. Jane and I accompanied Mum and Dad to his appointment and I popped in and out watching the ceremony in the waiting room. I was so desperate for Rami Malik to win an Oscar for best actor for his portrayal of Freddie Mercury in the movie *Bohemian Rhapsody*. I remember jumping up and down when his name was announced as the winner and running back to the ward to tell Dad. The other people in the waiting room looked up in amusement at my unbridled glee, and I had a giggle at home telling Ruby about this. I had loved Queen back in the day and I used to put my plastic, yellow, Sony cassette player in Mum and Dad's open bedroom window as a teenager and roller skate up and down the driveway to 'Bohemian Rhapsody'.

The day after he had chemo, Dad went to choir practice as usual and was in fine voice. Dad and Mum have been in the Silver Notes Choir for over twenty years, and they loved rehearsing each Tuesday afternoon at the Temperance Hall. We often used to have a laugh when Dad said, 'We are singing to the oldies at Lyndoch or Mercy this week.' Dad would most likely have been as old or older than the seniors he was singing to. I popped in to see them over the next couple of days, and Dad seemed fine. On Friday evening, Ruby stayed with her granny and pa Joe and Dad got up during the night and had a fall. Luckily, Ruby was there to help Mum get Dad back to bed.

The next morning, he wasn't looking at all well, and the decision was made to call an ambulance to take him to the hospital. It was a stinker of a day, about forty degrees Celsius, and we all met at the hospital fairly concerned about Dad. He was moved from the emergency ward to a bed in the palliative care ward quite late. Jane was adamant that he would need to be closely monitored as he would try to get out of bed, and she discussed this with the nursing staff. We went home feeling assured that he was in capable hands.

Before walking into Dad's hospital room the following morning, I glanced over at the wall outside, and I was sure that I saw a spray of blood. I dismissed this as being stupid and walked into the room. The scene that greeted me made me gasp. Dad was sitting up in bed with two black eyes and a large bump on his head. I was speechless and let out a sob. Mum and Jane followed me a couple of minutes later, and they too, stood in shock. I ran out of the room to ring Allan and tell him what had happened. We weren't given an explanation, really no-one knew how Dad had sustained his injuries, in a hospital, directly across from the nurses' station!

After this incident, Dad was not left alone again for one second. We all stayed with him in shifts around the clock, all day and all night. The following ten days were the worst ten days of my life. Dad lurched from one code blue to the next. Everything that could've gone wrong did go wrong. It was one disaster after another, and we knew that Dad was not going to recover and come home.

Dad loved a good sing-along; he had been singing all his life. We were gathered around his bed one night, and he started singing quite softly at first. We all joined in singing with him, I put in the harmonies to 'The Northern Lights of Old Aberdeen', and for hours

Dad sang like he was giving a performance at Carnegie Hall. He sang magnificently; my strong and totally irreplaceable Dad was giving his final performance.

*

Dad passed away with all the family around him on 14 March 2019. He was eighty-eight years old and had lived in Australia for sixty-two years. His funeral was held on Saturday, 23 March, at St John's Presbyterian Church here in Warrnambool, where he and Mum had married fifty-eight years before. Jane, Allan, and I wrote and read Dad's eulogy. The three of us did him proud, speaking about his life in three sections. I spoke about his life growing up in Scotland, Jane spoke about Dad moving to Australia and making a life and family here, and Allan spoke about his 'Pa Joe' years, being a much-loved grandfather to his six totally adored grandchildren.

The church was packed, and there wasn't a dry eye in the house. Ruby and I sang one of Dad's favourite songs, 'You Are My Sunshine,' and the Silver Notes Choir sang 'You Raise Me Up'. As Dad's coffin was carried from the church, a lone piper played 'Scotland the Brave'. I felt my heart breaking into a thousand pieces when I stood and watched as the hearse left the church and moved slowly down the street. I could still hear the pipes playing. There are certain times in your life where words can't express how you feel.

*

Nothing can prepare you for the death of a parent. Thank God Ruby was staying with me, and I had to do normal things like making cups of tea, have a shower, breathe in and out, and cook dinner. One Sunday, about three weeks after the funeral, Ruby and I decided to have a pyjama day and watch movies. I chose the Australian film

Ladies in Black. We started watching it, and I was loving the fact that it was set in Sydney in the 1950s at about the same time that Dad had emigrated to Australia. It was interesting to see the fashions of the time and the ladies wearing gloves and hats in Australia in summer *and* how difficult it was for non-Australians to assimilate into our way of life. Dad had loved the book, *They're a Weird Mob,* by Nino Culotta, which tells the story of an Italian guy emigrating to Australia in the nineteen sixties. The movie reminded me of this, and I was totally caught up in it.

I looked over at Ruby and said, 'Pa Joe would love this.' It was at that precise moment that I realised that my funny, exasperating, strong, stubborn, and entirely irreplaceable, beloved Dad—was dead! He would never be able to watch another movie with me, howl with laughter over Billy Connelly skits, discuss who sang the best on *The Voice* or laugh about *Mrs Brown's Boys.* I fell to the floor sobbing my heart out. Poor Ruby looked on, horrified, but understood that the penny had just dropped for me. My dad was gone forever.

I was drinking a lot. I even put vodka in my water bottle and pretended it was water. Ruby went to take a swig of it one night to wash down a tablet, but I snatched it out of her hand before she could drink it. I had a bottle stashed under the kitchen sink, one in my bedside drawer, and another one for emergencies. I was drinking about a bottle of vodka every two days and a bottle of wine every day as well. I had just had too much to deal with in such a short time, losing Dad, my fiancé, and being evicted from my home and having to find a new place to live.

Jane had written to the Warrnambool City Council to ask if we could put a memorial plaque on one of the new benches overlooking the beach. Dad had loved the promenade path next to Lady Bay Beach, and he walked along it nearly every day of his life in Warrnambool. They responded by saying that we could buy the bench and place the plaque on it provided we were happy to maintain it. We were all rapt with this outcome and felt that it was a very fitting tribute to our much-loved Pa Joe.

*

I was still doing my Zumba classes. I was a very fit alcoholic. I was in a state of just existing, going through the motions. I had dated a couple of men, but my excessive drinking would've turned anyone off. One guy was an acquaintance I had known for years, and I saw him several times. I enjoyed his company but came to realise that he didn't want a relationship, only the added benefits. I was slowly beginning to think that I deserved better than this, and for the first time in my entire life when the 'booty call' came, I said, 'No, I don't want to come over for a casual hook up because you just feel like having sex. I am better than that.' It felt very good to be empowered and honest and stand up for myself for a change!

I tried to cancel the registry office, reception, and honeymoon. I got a refund for some of the actual wedding expenses, but I couldn't get a refund for the trip. It was a ten-day, all expenses included stay at Coconut Island, off the coast of Phuket. I asked several friends if they would like to join me, but no-one was free to come. I decided to go and call it my 'me moon'. I am a well-seasoned traveller, so going alone didn't faze me.

I did email the resort and ask them not to do the flowers and champagne thing in my room, though. I got there quite late at night and walked into the suite. On the bed were two towels forming swans, their beaks touching and forming a love heart, with rose petals strewn all over the bed. A handwritten note said, 'Coconut Island welcomes the new Mr and Mrs Small. Congratulations from all of us here, and have a beautiful honeymoon.' They obviously didn't get my memo! The Thai people are gorgeous, though, and went out of their way to make sure I had everything I needed for a lovely holiday.

I befriended a couple of honeymoon couples, and they invited me to have drinks and sit by the pool with them. I told them the story of why I was here alone, and they were so kind and caring. I drank the 'free' cocktails until they came out my ears; I *was* drinking for two, after all! The food was mouth-watering, and the satay sticks were so delicious that I ate them every day. There were three restaurants in the resort to choose from. A little Thai waiter befriended me and made sure every morning that my favourite table overlooking the beach was free so I could eat my breakfast there. Before I left, I gave him a thank you card and some money to help him out. He burst into tears and hugged me.

I did a lot of reading and thinking about my life. I mentioned to one of the honeymoon couples that I had been a singer in a band in my heyday. One night they asked the house band if I could do a song with them. I got up and sang 'Blue Bayou'. It was lots of fun, and the band asked me to join them again the following night. We did some Cold Chisel stuff; all through my performing years, people have always yelled out 'do "Khe Sahn"' at the end of the night, so we did that. I had a good time on my 'me moon'. The only sad thing was returning to my flash honeymoon suite by myself every night. I amused myself by watching the Thai equivalent of *Neighbours* and making up what the actors were saying while drinking the minibar dry.

Once home in May 2019, I decided to volunteer some of my time at 'Food Share' to help struggling families who had difficulty affording basic food items. I also took a weekly shift at the Red Cross Op Shop, and I enjoyed talking to the customers and helping people select outfits for fancy dress parties. I had taken Dad's place in the choir and enjoyed wearing his Silver Notes jacket and singing from his lyrics book. I had lots of giggles reading his corrections and comments beside the songs. We were performing one afternoon at Lyndoch in Warrnambool, and we had started singing a Scottish song that Dad had always sung. I could hear him so clearly singing in my mind, and I felt his presence all around me. This has happened several times, and I know that Dad is close by watching and guiding me.

I was sitting on Pa Joe's memorial bench one day, thinking about my life and if I would ever meet a decent man again. I had just finished saying, 'There has to be *one* good bloke left on the planet, Dad, surely?' A guy sat down beside me. He was talking on his phone and had a Scottish accent. When he finished the call I asked, 'How long have you been in Australia?'

He replied, 'Only about six months.' He and his partner had made the move for work. We started chatting, and I told him about my dad and immigrating here in the fifties and that we were sitting on his memorial bench. It turned out that my new friend was also a 'Fifer' and came from a place about ten kilometres from where Dad's family had lived when he was a boy in Scotland. Walking back to my car, I looked up and said, 'You got the Scottish thing right, Dad, but can you make sure the next one is single and heterosexual?' He still hasn't shown up!

I was still drinking for Australia and doing my normal stuff. I went to see my doctor, and she was keen for me to go to detox. I was not keen on going to detox. I had already looked into a private rehab facility, but I wasn't prepared to pay ten grand or more. My GP talked me into doing a week at the local hospital, and I reluctantly agreed.

My dear friend Chris drove me to the hospital and reassured me that the week would pass quickly. At the traffic lights before the hospital, I was tempted to do a runner, but I knew that I had to face my addiction head-on. She kept glancing at me apprehensively because she knew how hard I was finding it to come face to face with my alcohol dependence. I took my doona and pillow with me for comfort and was admitted on a Monday morning in October 2019. I felt weird because I don't like hospitals very much, and this was a total admission that I had a severe problem with alcohol that required medical intervention. I couldn't pretend to myself any longer that I could moderate my alcohol intake or quit if I chose to. It was confronting and scary.

The disadvantage of living in a rural community like Warrnambool is that everyone knows everyone. One of my nurses was a friend's brother, and I was given the weekly menu by a lass that I had gone to high school with. She looked absolutely shocked when she came into my room. There were people in there with far more severe addictions than I had, but I decided to give it a fair go and do whatever was required of me. You weren't allowed to have your phone or any outside communication.

I befriended a young Koorie lass who had left her three kids at home to come to detox. It was eye-opening to hear other people's stories of addiction and the repercussions of substance abuse. It made me realise that I had been a high-functioning alcoholic, as I have never hit the rock bottoms and lost everything that several of my hospital companions had.

Sitting in my hospital room reading one day, I looked out the window and saw Adam walking by laughing with a mate. I was filled with anger and rage. He had not helped me at all. He had just belittled me and made me feel like a leper. It had been 'his way or the highway' the whole time we had been together. I know that I had not fared well in my last few relationships, but his total refusal to support and care for me was beyond my comprehension. I thought of getting my lipstick and writing *Adam Small is a weak and selfish prick* on my window for all to see. I didn't do this, but the thought of it was satisfying. I might get a bit more satisfaction yet!

I got a taxi home from the hospital, and I felt strange again. Over the course of my hospital stay, I had been forced to confront my alcohol addiction head-on and what I was going to do about it. I couldn't just 'sweep it under the rug' anymore. I had also been contemplating how much longer I could drink excessively without serious health implications. I was worried that I might have a fatty liver or have seriously reduced my life expectancy.

I didn't buy any alcohol for the first few days. I had a cask of red wine in the cupboard and drank one or two glasses with my evening meal. I resolved not to buy any vodka, gin, or white wine. I managed this and had cut my drinking in half very quickly. It was tricky when my family came for dinner on Tuesday nights. I hid my red wine glass behind a tray on the kitchen bench. I wasn't getting really pissed anymore, but I just couldn't shake the habit of 'Oh, it's five o'clock, time to have a wine.' The *wine-witch* and I have had a long-standing date for many years, and I knew that she wouldn't leave me alone without a fight.

I started thinking that it would be great to go to the UK again and see the relatives once more. I hopped online and began working out my retirement trip. Yes, I would make a retirement trip to all the places I loved or had wanted to visit all my life.

Mum had given me a photo of my granny when she was a little girl. Her family had been Irish and moved to Scotland early last century. They were staunch Irish Catholics, and when granny met my Scottish Protestant grandfather, there was going to be a problem. My granny fell pregnant with their child, and she was disowned by her family. Dad never met his maternal grandparents, but he knew that they had lived in Castleblayney in Ireland.

I have never been to Ireland before, so I decided to include it in my itinerary. I posted the photo of my granny's family on a Facebook site called 'Castleblayney Past and Present,' and a lovely lass called Sinead replied that the young man in my picture looked very much like her brother. We got chatting, and she was keen to meet me and show me around when I arrived in Castleblayney. We worked out that we probably weren't related after all, but we have adopted each other as cousins, which is such a lovely outcome.

Ruby was going to fly to London at the start of the winter school holidays and we were going to spend several days together sightseeing. Then we were going to fly up to Scotland to meet Mum and Jane in Kirkcaldy, Dad's hometown in Fife, Scotland, to celebrate what would have been his ninetieth birthday. All the Scottish rellies were going to attend, and we were very excited about this. Then a trip to Shetland with Ruby to show her where her great grandparents had lived.

*

I had always wanted to go to Prague since I had seen the haunting film clip of 'Never Tear Us Apart' by INXS. I was entranced by the old architecture, the romance of the Charles Bridge, and a brooding Michael Hutchence gliding past an old cemetery. I had booked several days to stay and explore there. I was flying to Athens and then taking the ferry to Mykonos and Santorini to holiday in beautiful traditional, white-washed Greek houses. My trip was all booked and paid for—no caravan parks or dodgy rooms in old *pensiones* this time. I was flying directly to Paris on 14 June 2020, staying in a traditional Parisian Haussmann apartment near the Champs-Élysées for five nights. I had booked dinner at the Eiffel Tower and a show at the Moulin Rouge. Six whole weeks on the adventure of a lifetime; I was beyond excited.

Anyone experiencing personal difficulties, please ring Lifeline Australia on 13 11 14.

Chapter 18
COVID and chaos

I rocked up to my op shop shift one Tuesday morning, and my lovely co-worker Cheryl said, 'Hey Margy, I just heard on the wireless that the Louvre in Paris has closed because of this bloody virus.'

I responded with, 'Unless they close all the airports and ground all the planes, I am still going, Cheryl.'

I enjoyed working with Cheryl, who has a wicked and very 'Aussie' sense of humour. We had hit it off from day one.

I had just finished booking my final flight home for the trip from Athens to Melbourne via Singapore when the shit hit the fan. I had spent about ten grand by then because I wanted to do it in style this time. No travel insurance companies would insure me against COVID-19, so I just took my chances that the situation wouldn't get any worse and I would still be able to go. Nope, the universe wouldn't even allow me to have a well-deserved retirement trip. I was pissed off but then realised that there were many people in a far worse predicament than me. Watching the news was quite startling, and very quickly, the pandemic was totally shutting down the entire world.

Suddenly we were confined to our homes. Schools, shops, churches and businesses shut down. There wasn't one organisation or one person who wasn't affected by COVID-19. There was no choir practice, the op shop was closed, and the streets were bare and quiet. I continued doing my volunteering at Food Share but had to wear a

191

mask and remain one and a half metres from my co-workers. Poor Mum was confined to her house and really struggled with not being able to do her activities or hug people. My lovely mum is definitely a 'hugger', and it was tough getting used to the 'elbow' and 'hip bump' greeting that was replacing handshakes and hugs.

Jane, Allan, and I visited daily with her groceries and took turns doing her messages, but she was really feeling isolated and alone. No more family dinners here on Tuesday nights and Zumba classes were cancelled. Life as we had always known it was cancelled. As a post on Facebook said, it was like the universe collectively sending us to our rooms for a long, hard think about things.

Mum has a little cavoodle called Lottie. She was born on the day Dad died and has been with Mum since she was a puppy. Mum started letting Lottie spend a couple of nights a week with me for the company because I was very lonely. She just really liked me, and I thought she was cute, too. Lottie was my saviour throughout the long weeks and months of lockdown. She would sit on my lap and watch Netflix with me. We would walk along the beach for miles, snuggle under the blankets on cold winter nights and just hang out together. One little dog made so much difference in my life. Lottie taught me what unconditional love looks like. One night when I went to the kitchen to get my sixth wine refill, I swear that she looked at me and shook her head. When I came back into the lounge room, she stood up, looked straight at me, and slowly sashayed down to the end of the couch and plopped herself down. I thought it was very amusing, but it did make me stop and think that even Lottie thought I drank too much.

I was very lonely and getting quite bored. I saw an ad about studying at TAFE and read through the courses on offer online. They were offering a midyear intake in the commercial cookery course, so I decided to enrol in this course. I had always loved cooking, and in my teaching years, it had been my relaxation after a hard day at school. I would come home and flit about the kitchen with my wine glass within reach and take out my frustrations on the onions and carrots. I felt rather proud wearing my new chef's gear and opening my chef's knives kit for the first time. There were about ten other people in my class, and they seemed like a nice bunch.

I learnt a lot in the first few weeks and obtained a whole new respect for chefs and people employed in the food service industry. It was gruelling standing on a concrete floor cooking for hours on end. Not being a young thing anymore, I would arrive home from my day at chef school totally stuffed and hardly able to move. I was enjoying my studies, but my back wasn't, so I deferred my place until the beginning of 2021. Our end-of-year breakup was a bus trip around the 'foodie' attractions of the southwest regions of Victoria. The first port of call was at a chocolate factory in Cobden, where I'd had my first teaching placement all those years ago. I sat looking out the bus window on the way there, and I could still remember the houses and landmarks clearly. I thought about how strange life is, and that I had come around in a complete circle.

During the long, lonely months of COVID lockdown, I did a lot of thinking about what I wanted the rest of my life to look like. I had come to terms with living alone and caring for myself. I could feel something inside me shifting very slightly, and I wasn't sure what it was. It felt like a tiny little light that was flickering and reminding me that my life wasn't over yet, that I still had so much to give and live for. Sitting on the couch watching Netflix and drinking every night was just getting tiresome. I hated feeling groggy in the mornings and sleeping poorly. I would run to the loo after drinking my red wine and just make it most times. The wine shits are revolting. I was sick of cleaning the loo!

My friend Chris also lives alone, and we supported each other during the pandemic. Chris has been a friend of mine for years and had sadly lost her husband, Peter, suddenly in 2015. Her late hubby was at high school with Bill and me, and they used to love coming to see our band playing. I admired her courage and resilience in continuing her journey alone even though she was a heartbroken young widow. She was quite concerned about my drinking and told me so. She was correct in saying that when I was drinking I was not the best version of myself. I was thinking about all of this, and one night in October, I thought, *What if I don't drink tonight? I am sure that the roof won't fall in and the sun will rise tomorrow.* Ruby came for tea, which made it easier because I hadn't drunk alcohol in front of her for a long time. The next day I saw a message about 'The 30-Day Alcohol Experiment', which is an online experiment to abstain from alcohol for thirty days. This was being discussed on my Club Soda Alcohol-Free group page. Someone had posted that they had done it and said that it had changed their life. I was really sceptical about this, but I decided that I had nothing to lose and a lot to gain.

I got out my 'quit lit' and *This Naked Mind* by Annie Grace and read it again. For anyone who wants to stop drinking alcohol, I highly recommend reading this book because it made a lot of sense to me, and I liked Annie's non-preachy and warm approach to sobriety. Annie Grace has also written *The Alcohol Experiment: A 30-day, Alcohol-Free Challenge to Interrupt Your Habits and Help You Take Control*, and I started reading about it. I signed up that day to do thirty days without alcohol. I felt that I needed to see if my life would improve without drinking and if I could actually go that long without drinking. The first couple of days were rough. I did a Zumba workout and felt light-headed and threw up. My heart was beating arrhythmically, I was sweating, shaking and I had a headache. I rang to make a doctor's appointment and got in.

My wonderful, long-suffering GP was so happy when I told her that I was trying to give up the grog, she nearly fell off her chair! My doctor had been advising me to cut down on the grog for many years. She prescribed naltrexone tablets daily for me to take. This drug helps with the alcohol cravings which I needed after drinking for so long. I was given a referral to have my blood work done and check to make sure that my liver was functioning properly. I was very pleased and relieved to get good results on my next visit. Everything was in the normal range; even my liver was okay, which I was thrilled about.

I continued my thirty-day quest to abstain from drinking, and I was surprised that I could go without drinking. I followed the alcohol experiment and journalled how I was feeling every day and the changes that I was noticing. I joined the online 'Alcohol Experiment' forum and found the people very supportive, and I began to post daily about my sober journey. I made friends, and we swapped stories about the things that worked for us in our desire to become alcohol-free. I replaced my date with the wine-witch at five o'clock with a walk or a 'mocktail' which I made from juice, limes, and ginger ale. I started to feel so much better about myself. I was sleeping better, my anxiety had reduced, and I was enjoying my sober life. I was walking along the beach one day with Lottie, and an incredible feeling of happiness and relief washed over me. I felt like I had walked out of a black and white movie into dazzling technicolour. I now know that this is called a 'pink cloud' experience, and many people experience this when they first give up alcohol.

Chapter 19
What now?

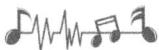

After my Nanna passed away in 1995, I went to see a clairvoyant because I was very upset that I wasn't there with her when she died. Nanna had always said to me that she could 'hear me speaking' when she read my letters that I had written to her when I had been overseas. I have been an avid letter writer all my life, and even as a young woman, I was always writing letters. I would tell Sally and Sandy that I had 'written a letter' over the weekend, and they would say, 'Was it a happy letter, or what are you pissed off about now?'

Letter-writing was my way of getting my thoughts and feelings down on paper. The clairvoyant asked me if I was a writer, and I said, 'No, but I have been writing reports today.'

She said, 'No, you are a writer and one day you will write a book.'

I laughed out loud and said, 'Okay, I hope I am not as busy as I am right now; I barely have enough time to go to the loo, let alone time to write a book.'

She said, 'You will write one, and it will be very successful.' She also told me that I have already met my soulmate and that it wasn't Bill. I have pondered this many times over the past twenty-five years, but I can't work out who it might be? She said that Nanna was there with her and told me that I will have many challenges to face in my lifetime but that I would be strong enough to cope with them.

*

It is a strange thought that all of my life experiences have led me to this point in time. I guess that I could've just sat in my comfy chair in the lounge room of my little rented unit and told everyone to piss off and leave me alone. I know what hard experiences I have lived through, and no-one would blame me if all I wanted to do now was sit quietly patting Lottie and licking my wounds.

A friend of mine said, 'You have had a lot of shit thrown at you in your life, Margy, but you have chosen to use it to become stronger. You are a phoenix rising from the ashes, not a bloody victim.' I must say that I like that image, and I do want to share my experiences in the hope that other women will be empowered to do the same.

Everyone has choices! We choose our friends, our occupations, and our willingness to participate actively or passively in life. Our attitude shapes the way we view the world. When my life became difficult, I just thought about getting through one day at a time. I have found that once you are doing something instead of thinking about it, things seem easier to cope with. There is always hope. I like to think of myself as an optimist, and a 'glass is always half full' person.

I believe that people feel more comfortable when they can pigeonhole others into a certain role. I have been quite surprised about the reaction I have received when I tell people that I no longer drink. I think this scares some people because you are stepping out of the role they assigned you. It also holds up a mirror to their own habits and behaviour, which is rather confronting to them.

In writing this book, I have had to step *way* outside my comfort zone. I have wrestled with being so open and honest. I have copped some flack about this. 'Why are you going to publish it? I can understand why you wrote it, but publishing it is a bit crazy.' I actually did decide to can it at one point after this pressure got a bit too much. I was working at my laptop at the end of my dining room table where I am writing right now and looked up and said out loud, 'Okay, Nanna, Poppa, Dad, Sandy, and Sally, if you want me to do this, give me a sign.' On this particular day, I was going to attend the March 4 Justice on the Civic Green here in Warrnambool. Our fair city is not a place where people protest very often; it is a very conservative, rural city. I promised my friend who organised it that I would go because she was worried that there would be about five people and her dog there.

I drove downtown, and I couldn't get a park near the Civic Green. I thought this was very strange on a Monday at lunchtime. I ended up parking two blocks away on a friend's nature strip and I walked back. I stopped in my tracks in disbelief when I arrived to see over a thousand people, men, women, students, professional people, and children, crowded onto the green with large banners saying, #ENOUGH and I Believe Her and Use Your Voice. I was totally gobsmacked!

A lady about my age looked very scared as she got up to speak to the crowd. My friend held her hand to support and encourage her as she told us that she had been sexually assaulted by three different men by the age of twelve. She had been brave and reported these offences and gone through the harrowing court process for her perpetrators only to be given a 'slap on the wrist'. I had tears rolling down my face listening to the pain and anguish in her voice, and I looked up and nodded because I had been given my sign.

I came home with a renewed sense of purpose and sat down and completed this book. I wrote with confidence, conviction, and courage! Yes, it is time to say #ENOUGH and to be unashamed to tell our stories. I have lived with shame and fear for too long. I have owned my past, and this has given me freedom and the key to my future. I will never be scared or ashamed ever again!

Chapter 20
You have always had the power, my dear

I have experienced the whole gamut of emotions writing this book, from fear to love, joy to despair, and misery to total bliss. I have had *high highs and low lows* in reflecting upon my journey so far. It has certainly been a bumpy and interesting ride, to say the least. A 'rollicking adventure, hen', as my Scottish aunty put it.

I have been contemplating the idea of happiness and what that means. For us mortals, I think it is a very fleeting state, and we only experience it in small glimpses. I was chatting to Jim about this the other day, and he agreed with my observation. Even in some of the darkest moments of my life, I have managed to find a tiny nugget of joy to sustain me. In this last month or so, while I was struggling with my 'why', as in 'why are you publishing this book?' I have had to dig deep. The naysayers have come out in force, and self-doubt is a specialty of mine. It would've been so easy to stop, tuck the manuscript away in my bottom drawer, and just be satisfied that I had purged my story.

This book and its message are bigger than me. I am one little person in a world of billions of little people. I have always believed that I am quite an insignificant part of this world. It takes a lot of those 'little people' to create change and have the courage to speak up. I was reading about Greta Thunberg, and I thought to myself, *What if she had said to herself, 'I am only a teenager, I don't even have a university degree, what possible difference or change can I make?'* She was brave; she followed her heart and the power of her convictions and spoke up. Greta has created change on a global scale.

I have dealt with a lot of change in my lifetime, professionally, personally, and emotionally. I think that this has made me a very resilient person. As a teacher, I went from writing on a blackboard with chalk to computers and smartboards in my classrooms. I have had to say goodbye to homes that I loved and relationships that I invested my heart and soul into. I had to build up strength and courage to overcome feelings of unworthiness, loneliness, abuse, betrayal, and abandonment. It is very difficult to feel 'worthy' when you have experienced so much trauma.

I have been learning to set boundaries to protect myself from hurt. I wore my heart on my sleeve for many years, and it is quite bruised and battered. Having low self-esteem encourages others to treat you however they see fit. I am not prepared to cop that anymore. I have been standing up for myself and calling out 'crap' behaviour when I see it. This is a very different way of living for me, but one that is necessary if I am going to go forward being my true self.

In Dad's eulogy, Allan spoke of people often not being their authentic selves. He went on to say that in Dad's final days in the hospital, we saw him as he really was—cheeky, honest, and hilariously funny. One morning, a nurse walked into Dad's room, and he said, 'You look magnificent,' in his broad Scottish accent. Dad left us being his authentic self. I hope that I will be confident enough to be my authentic self from now on. I have pretended to be so many other people in my life. I am happy to now be Margy Jackson, warts and all.

Since Dad passed away, I have walked on the beach a lot. I bought a bodyboard and a wetsuit, and I go to the beach most days. I hadn't been out surfing since I was a teenager. I don't look anything like that nubile young lass, but I couldn't care less! It is so peaceful and soothing paddling around in the sea. I do this right in front of Dad's bench, and I know that he would be sitting there grinning in his orange fluoro jumper and feeling so proud of me.

My incredible children were here for dinner last weekend. Jim jumped on the train in Melbourne and came home to see me because I was feeling quite sad about things. I cooked one of their favourites: slow-cooked roast lamb. Jim said that it was worth the trip from Melbourne just to eat Mum's roast lamb. This special time together brought back happy memories of many Saturday night dinners while my kids were growing up. It was the one night of the week where I would set the table nicely, and we would all sit down and share a delicious meal, talk and laugh and enjoy each other's company. I sat in my chair and watched my kind, thoughtful and loving children together, and my heart nearly burst with joy. It was so wonderful to be sober and present in their company. I am the luckiest mum in the world, and my two children are the loves of my life.

My lovely next-door neighbour invited me out for a coffee with a good friend of hers recently. This beautiful lady happened to be the mum of the little boy who was the lead performer in my *Superheroes* production all those years ago. He is now a principal of a school himself, and she told me that every year his school have a big musical production. She said, 'You are a legend in our house, Margy, for instilling such a love of music and the performing arts in my boys.' I was very humbled to hear this, and it made me feel like I have made a difference in people's lives.

I also hope this *book* will make a difference in people's lives and encourage other women who have struggled with substance abuse, anxiety and depression, and domestic violence to also use their voices to speak out. I am only one of many, and we must start having these conversations openly if anything is going to change. It *is* bloody scary to make yourself vulnerable and be brave enough to speak up. We must start having these real conversations and being honest if change is going to occur. It is so liberating and healing to stop being afraid

203

and ashamed. Accepting yourself and being honest is the first step in healing and moving forwards.

In conclusion, I will leave you with an update about all the wonderful people who have shaped my life and allowed me to share my stories with you. Joanne, my childhood neighbour, and I are still friends; the 'girls' from Queensland and I caught up for our thirtieth reunion in Brisbane in September 2018. We had a brilliant weekend looking at our old photos and laughing about our exploits as young backpackers in Europe in 1988. My incredible UK rellies were so disappointed that we couldn't make it over to see them last year because of COVID-19. We are currently replanning our trip for when we have had our COVID jabs, and it is safe to travel again.

My beautiful mum is happily hugging everyone once more, and she continues to be the most selfless and loving person that I have ever met. I learnt from the best! Many thanks must go to my wonderful family for allowing me to share my memories of Dad and us growing up. Without their support, I simply wouldn't be here typing this right now.

I woke up early this morning, and I had tears running down my face. I am not sure if this is because I am glad that I have finally finished writing this book or if I am grateful and relieved that I am still here. My emotions have come flooding back since I stopped drinking. I had masked my feelings with alcohol for so long. Yesterday, I received a parcel in the mail. It was a ring that I had purchased online. The ring says, *I am enough*. Three simple words that I can now look at and believe. From this day onwards, I will look at my ring and see someone who has been through the toughest of times and survived them. I do have a voice, and I have used it to write this book. I am a work in progress, and I am far from perfect. But I finally do know: I *am* enough!

You have always had the power, my dear

THE END!

For anyone experiencing personal difficulties, please call:
Lifeline Australia: 13 11 14
Beyond Blue Australia: 1300 224 636
Suicide Call Back Service: 1300 659 467
Domestic Violence Australia: 1800 737 732 (1800 RESPECT).

I *am* enough!

Margy Jackson
December 2021
www.margyjackson.com

CPSIA information can be obtained
at www.ICGtesting.com
Printed in the USA
BVHW042327130322
631391BV00009B/547